TEACHER APPRAISAL
AND
SELF-EVALUATION:

A PRACTICAL GUIDE

Robert Hancock and David Settle

BLACKWELL EDUCATION

For Lyndsey and Linda

First published 1990

Published by Basil Blackwell Ltd
108 Cowley Road
Oxford OX4 1JF
England

British Library Cataloguing in Publication Data
Hancock, Robert
 Teacher appraisal and self-evaluation: a practical guide.
 1. Teachers. Self-evaluation
 I. Title   II. Settle, David
 371.144

ISBN 0–631–17444 3 (hb)
ISBN 0–631–17445 1 (pb)
Typeset in Linotron 202
by Best-set Typesetter Limited, Hong Kong
Printed in Great Britain by Dotesios Printers Ltd, Trowbridge

Acknowledgements

We would like to record our sincere thanks to Linda Settle for undertaking all the typing of our draft material, and for losing chapter 7. In addition, our thanks go to both Linda and Lyndsey for putting up with all our little idiosyncrasies throughout the production of the book.

Contents

Introduction

Teachers have always appraised their work. This is reflected in the levels of staffroom discussion on teaching and learning, the time committed to lesson preparation and marking, and teachers' determined efforts to develop professionally through in-service training.

However, the appraisal process has too often been purely informal, unstructured and unrecorded. The contribution that appraisal makes to the quality of education has tended to be implicit rather than formal, structured and explicit.

The implementation of the 1988 Education Reform Act changed this situation. The provision of teacher appraisal is now considered a formal requirement.

The major vehicle for developing teacher appraisal was the School Teacher's Appraisal Pilot Study which started in six LEAs in January 1987. This Study followed the publication of the Advisory Conciliation and Arbitration Service (ACAS) Working Group Report in June 1986. The Report of the pilot study highlighted a number of key elements in the teacher-appraisal process:

- an initial meeting between appraiser and appraisee
- self-appraisal by the appraisee
- classroom observation
- collection of data from other sources agreed with the appraisee
- an appraisal interview, in which professional targets for action are agreed
- the preparation of an appraisal statement to be agreed by both parties
- follow-up, including a formal review meeting.

These elements were seen by the pilot study groups as stages in a cycle. The full cycle of appraisal may extend over a period of up to two years.

This book addresses *all aspects* of the proposed process and lays great stress on understanding: the overall appraisal process, the relationship and interactions between appraisers and appraisees, and the crucial role of self-appraisal.

In the Cambridge Institute of Education's Evaluation Report on the pilot scheme, great emphasis was placed on self-appraisal and the teacher participant's reactions to self-appraisal. The report says:

During the period of the pilot study, the importance of self-appraisal has been generally recognised even though, in some cases, it has been 'difficult to promote'.

For some, self-appraisal was the most significant part:

The whole process wouldn't have been much without it.

We feel that self-appraisal provides the most important opportunity for the kind of professional reflection which leads to positive change.

The difficulties of promoting self-appraisal referred to above appear to reflect a number of factors: insufficient training, insufficient time and insufficient overall understanding.

However, the position we take in this book sets the role of self-appraisal at the heart of teacher appraisal. Such self-appraisal demands that teachers gain an insight into their own performance and collect personal evidence of the quality of their work. In chapter 5 we set out in detail a range of tools and practical procedures for self-appraisal. These will not only give teachers access to details of their own working practice but also challenge them to look at the point they have reached in the development of their skills, knowledge and understanding, and their relationships with pupils and peers. It is our belief that quality performance in the classroom is the crucial aspect of effectiveness for teachers, and many of the strategies provided in this book focus upon classroom practice.

Education has been in a process of fundamental and rapid change. However, one key aspect of teaching remains unchanged: the commitment of teachers to provide for the development of the pupils in their care. At a time of change it is important to retain self-confidence in personal strengths, and to identify any shortcomings with honesty as a basis for development needs.

This book is written with this in mind and we feel confident that it will significantly both help those who read it and apply its procedures, and provide a framework for all aspects of a formal appraisal scheme.

Throughout the book we have used 'she' for consistency of style, but we recognise that this reference could equally well be 'he'.

Robert Hancock
David Settle
October 1989

Using this book

Who is it for?

Though many schools already operate schemes of teacher appraisal, there is much still to be developed. These developments will affect all teachers (appraisees), some teachers (appraisers), all headteachers and other senior managers in schools (teacher managers/appraisers), specialist staff responsible for staff development (staff development tutors), and advisers/inspectors/officers who will be charged with monitoring and evaluating the schemes.

How can it be used?

Appraisees

I want to know what teacher appraisal is — Read chapters 1, 2 and 4.

I want to know what I can expect in an
appraisal interview   — Read chapter 3.

I want to know what I can actually do — Read chapters 3, 5 and 6.

What's the point of teacher appraisal? — Read chapter 7.

Are there other things I should know? — Yes — read chapter 4 again.

Appraisers

I need to know about the theoretical background of teacher appraisal   — Read chapters 1 and 2.

I want to prepare well for the appraisal
interviews   — Read chapter 3.

I want to help my colleagues to gain a
clearer insight into the quality of their
own work   — Read chapters 5 and 6.

I want to help my colleagues see how
they and their work fit into the overall
work of the school   — Read chapter 4.

I want to know what we should expect
to gain from all this extra work   — Read chapter 7.

Teacher managers

I need to tell my governors why we have
a teacher-appraisal scheme — Read chapter 1.

Are there different ways of organising
appraisal? — Read chapter 2.

I want everyone to have a fair deal and
experience a consistent process — Read chapter 3.

Some of my staff want to work with each
other to gain a view of the quality of their
own work — Read chapters 4, 5 and 6

Advisers/inspectors

I need to have a clear basis for judging
the quality of schools' appraisal systems — Read chapters 1, 2 and 3.

I need to support teachers in my general
schools who want ideas on how to judge
the quality of their own work — Read chapters 4, 5 and 6.

I want some ideas on tools for collecting
objective evidence of teaching quality — Read chapter 5

Ideally the whole book should be read as a single text and the sequence of chapters is designed to present a natural development leading to a detailed scheme for supporting self-appraisal.

Fundamentally the book is planned to support teachers' practice through self-appraisal but its content should be helpful to all the other listed categories.

1 Where do I start?

What is appraisal?

It is much easier to be critical than correct — B Disraeli.

Appraisal goes on all the time at present. Teachers continually appraise the work that they do:

- that was a good lesson
- I am delighted with those examination results
- the class has behaved excellently today.

Those in posts of responsibility also continually appraise the work of 'their' staff:

- Mike's tutorial group has been very noisy recently
- Jean's pupil records were due in yesterday
- a poor set of lesson plans from Dave this week.

As a natural part of working life all teachers (including incentive allowance holders and headteachers) continually appraise themselves and each other. On the basis of such appraisal teachers 'rate' their own abilities, performance and potential, and teacher managers 'rate' those of the staff working for them.

Whilst much of the appraisal which goes on in this way can be helpful, it is often not based on objective information and can too often be an individual subjective judgement unclouded by appropriate evidence.

This form of appraisal is best termed 'informal' as it has few structures, does not work to agreed criteria, and has no formal recording mechanism. At its worst it can lead to inaccurate judgements being made on the value and quality of individuals and, with the 'confidential' reference system which is still prevalent within the country, can lead to an inappropriate blocking of an individual's promotion prospects.

Remember
We are all guilty of making inappropriate, subjective judgements of one another at different times.

Remember
In people we like, we can excuse anything. In people we don't like, anything is an excuse.

During the past twenty years performance appraisal within organisations has become common practice. It is an integral part of the vast majority of private industries, many public controlled industries and the civil service. Its use is now also common practice in many universities and colleges. Schools have, however, managed in the main to ignore appraisal. This could be considered understandable and quite correct if one notes our earlier comments and considers the concept of appraisal as being the 'old fashioned' one whereby the superior passed judgement, in isolation, on the personal worth of a subordinate.

Many teachers and teacher associations would argue that this form of appraisal still exists widely in education. We have mentioned the clearest example, namely that of references provided by headteachers. Such references are often provided when the writer has little or no direct knowledge of the employee's teaching ability.

A formal appraisal system must take teachers away from the dangers of such an informal system. At the end of an appraisal system a teacher should be able to answer the following questions accurately:

Yes, the Head says she is supporting me strongly.

- can I evaluate accurately the quality or otherwise of my work performance?
- can I match my skills appropriately to the different aspects of the job?
- do I recognise my own present and future training needs?
- am I able to select a career path appropriately?
- do I feel more motivated to do my job?

Where an appraisal system also involves a teacher's manager, the teacher, at the end of the process, should also recognise the manager as a person who is striving to help her to achieve both her own and the school's objectives.

Why do we need appraisal?

It's a good thing to have people size yer up wrong: Whin they've got yer measure ye'er in danger — Finley Peter Dunne (1919)

It would be far easier to write a chapter stating why we did not need appraisal!

One of the oldest and most frequently used arguments for not implementing an appraisal system in schools is that of size. How often do we hear comments such as:

- We're more like a family.
- I take pride in running a happy group.
- I know and work with every member of staff.

It must be argued that in a small staff setting poor management or one or two dissenters can destroy the work of the whole organisation, and also that small organisations are very open to mismanagement through personality management rather than professional organisation. Efficient management, including the need for a formal appraisal scheme, is just as important in the small organisation as it is in the large one.

We need appraisal for two main reasons:

- to be fair to all teaching staff (rather than unfairly holding secret views)
- to improve the quality of teaching and learning for all learners within the education system.

Without making any judgements on the particular system that is chosen we can identify the main reasons for the need for a performance appraisal system for an *individual teacher*. (We shall deal with the needs of the school later.)

The individual teacher should be able to:

How do you feel about appraisal?

- evaluate accurately the quality or otherwise of work performance
- match skills appropriately to the different aspects of the job
- recognise her own training needs for present and future
- select an appropriate career path.

If a teacher is able to gain success in the aspects mentioned the key outcome should be enhanced *motivation*.

We also need appraisal to help the school and LEA to become more efficient and to meet goals. It also has the same two prime intentions:

- to be fair to all teaching staff
- to improve the quality of teaching and learning.

The combination of needs from the teacher, school and LEA provide the *context* for the appraisal systems. We need appraisal systems to ensure that the education system as a whole meets its targets whilst supporting the staff within it.

When we see performance appraisal in context we can believe that both the individual teacher and the Local Education Authority have the same aims, an improvement in the quality of teaching and learning for individual learners, but we can clearly see a whole range of problems and pressures that will impinge on the establishment and running of any system. The following diagram gives an indication of the different factors which will impinge on an appraisal scheme.

performance appraisal		
CONTEXT	<u>School/LEA context</u> governors headteachers advisers/inspectors	<u>Teacher context</u> classroom staffroom individual learner
<u>GENERAL AREA</u> <u>OF CONCERN</u>	maintenance of organisational control institutional quality institutional results client satisfaction	utilization of resources quality of teaching/learning quality of relationships
<u>EXAMPLES OF</u> <u>PRACTICAL</u> <u>ASPECTS</u> <u>INVOLVED</u>	selection training manpower planning economic control public relations	employment legislation union pressure pay restraint government interference rights of the individual

Perhaps, therefore, the first question to ask is, 'What kind of changes would one hope to effect if one used an appraisal system?' Although the response is likely to be different for each individual it would appear appropriate to consider the responses on three levels:

- the teacher
- the teacher manager
- the school or LEA.

Denys John[1] took a refreshingly simple view in saying that appraisal is to do with planning one's work and the work of those for whom one is responsible. He states that at its simplest an appraisal system will help the individual to:

- plan and control her work better
- learn from mistakes and profit from successes
- co-ordinate her work with the work of others with whom she teaches.

If we then become more specific in approach we can combine the ideas of McGregor[2] and Stewart[3] and say that from an appraisal system the teacher and teacher manager should feel she has:

- greater insight into the job she has to do
- a better idea of where the job fits into the rest of the organisation
- an increased awareness of factors on which her performance is assessed
- an increased ability to monitor her own progress/performance
- the opportunity to ask questions in a free atmosphere
- a realisation of what she needs in the way of training and development.

For the school (headteacher and governors) and LEA many of the above will also apply. However, we need to ask about the specific items of relevance to this senior management group.

The following three items are the most significant. This group should:

- have a better understanding of the resources available to it
- have thought about how it measures the performance of its staff
- have given additional consideration to how it does its own job.

The school as an organisation needs an appraisal system to:

- improve performance
- enhance planning
- prevent problems.

In summation, there are three key reasons for needing an appraisal system:

- as a means of letting you know how you are doing, indicating to you the changes needed in behaviour, attitudes, skills and knowledge
- to provide you with an accurate base on which to build coaching, counselling or self-help schemes
- to ensure that objective judgements are made about you on which salary increases, promotions, transfers or job changes can be based.

What is the terminology?

Whilst we have used some of the words before reaching this section, we shall now indicate some of the terminology used in appraisal, and will ourselves use the terms, initials or acronyms as we continue through the book. As with all systems, appraisal has built up a specialist jargonised vocabulary. Some different systems also use the same words in different ways. We shall provide definitions for ours and then stick to them throughout the book.

PA —	Performance Appraisal.
PAS —	Performance Appraisal System.
TM —	Teacher Manager — any scale post-holder, senior, deputy or headteacher who has a person management role. It is of course possible (and frequently happens) for a TM to be both teacher and TM at the same time.
PA informal —	All managers tend to appraise their subordinates from time to time and in a number of ways without a formal framework. This is the informal approach.
PA formal —	Managers, well acquainted with the work of the appraisee, and working to a set schedule, fill in standard documents at set intervals (usually once per six months or twelve months). This is the formal approach.
Appraiser —	The person making the judgement or appraisal.
Appraisee —	The person being judged or appraised.
Open systems —	When the appraisees are shown their completed appraisal forms (no hidden records).
Closed systems —	When the appraisal forms are not shown to the appraisees even if they are informed of certain points during an appraisal interview.
Appraisal interview —	A formal meeting where the appraiser informs the appraisee of the outcome of the appraisal.

What are the dangers?

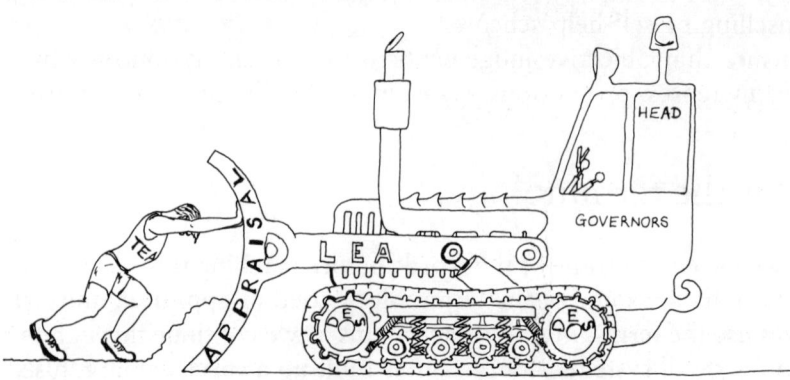

The major dangers involved in using an appraisal system can be grouped into three main problem areas:

- resistance to appraisal
- operational problems
- incompatibility.

The diagram below gives an indication of the main dangers involved:

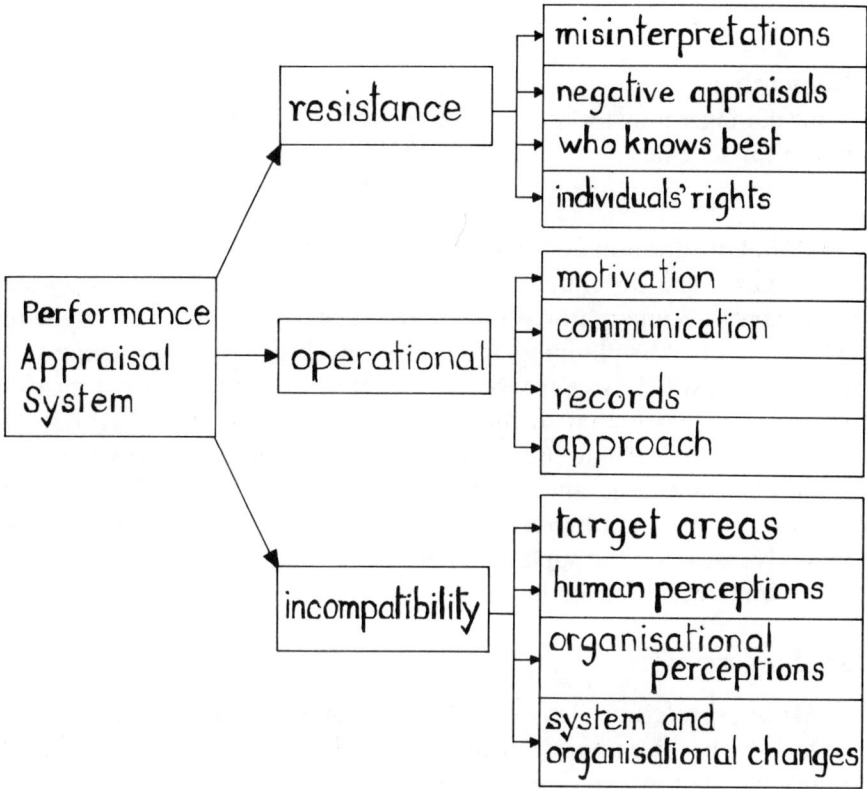

The 'resistance' area combines the human and personal traits which might mitigate against successful appraisal.

'Operational' contains elements which involve differing methods or approaches to appraisal systems.

'Incompatibility' contains items which are involved in tying together differing perceptions towards appraisal.

Remember
In this section we are really dealing with perceived THREATS and STRESS.

In looking at the 'resistance' area it is important to remember that some of the most serious resistance to appraisal systems can come from managers who, even if they agree with the concept, may well balk at the process. It is well accepted that many managers dislike criticising colleagues, or may not have the skills to cope with interviewing colleagues. Certainly some managers may also perceive the issue as an additional threat to their own status if they are to be judged on their own effective implementation of a scheme.

Remember
Your manager may feel under as much threat as you do because of an appraisal scheme.

Within education many of the insistances of the employees to retain their 'rights' as independent professionals are also strongly supported by managers. Some major points here are: recognition of the right to disagree, control by planning and not by checking, and management by reciprocal trust. McGregor would agree that one of the strongest cases the employee has is that of the assumption that the individual herself knows, or can learn, more than anyone else about her own needs, capabilities, strengths and weaknesses. This form of thinking would obviously provide strong resistance to an appraisal system which, even implicitly, said that the superior knew enough about the subordinate to decide what was best for her.

Key danger points

A   *Misinterpretation.* This can often occur when the appraisee does not feel she has been a part of the appraisal system. It is suggested that this occurs, in the main, when managers are resistant to or uncomfortable with the plan and, therefore, conduct any interviews in such a manner as to be unrecognisable as an appraisal format.

Remember
Resistance to any form of appraisal should be expected when a negative appraisal occurs.

B   *Motivation.* One of the major problems of an appraisal system can be the records that are offered. It is a matter of whether, in the long term, the records provide a positive or negative reinforcement.

Hertzberg[4] provides an interesting input to this discussion with his hygiene versus motivators argument. He feels that positive reinforcement should be provided by 'motivator factors' which would be intrinsic to the job. These would include such things as: the work itself, responsibility, and recognition for achievement. Negative factors would be provided by 'hygiene' factors which are extrinsic to the job and might include: working conditions, security, salary and supervision. The argument being made is obviously for an appraisal system which provides an extra step towards job enrichment.

C   *Incompatible target areas.* Any appraisal system will seek to achieve a range of different objectives (targets). The diagram below indicates just a few that might be involved:

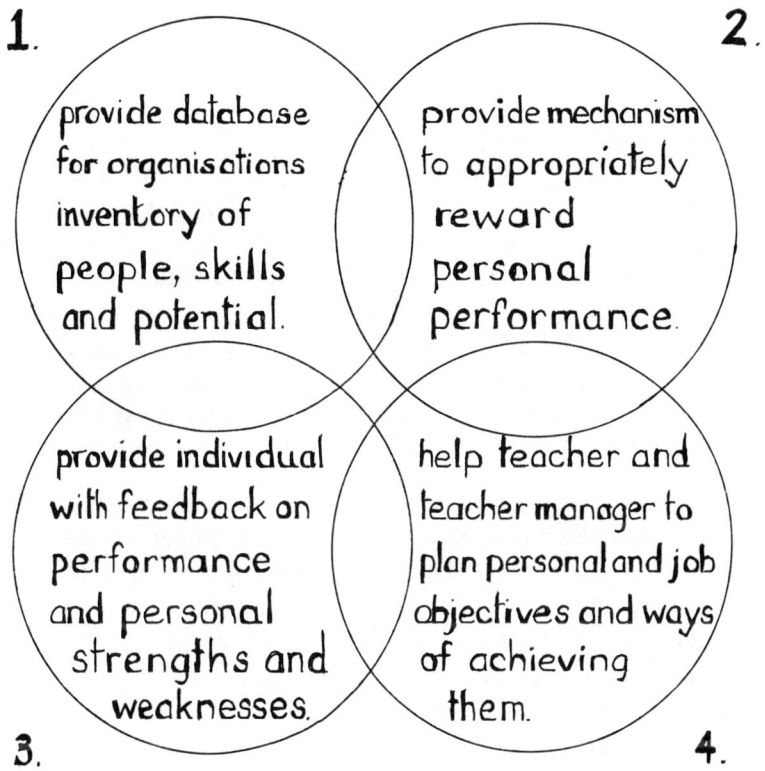

Ideally all four targets should be able to be achieved in harmony if true success is to be gained.

However:

- Target 1 may be incompatible with targets 3 or 4 if it is perceived as a control and not a development mechanism.
- Target 2 may be unconnected to 1, 3 or 4 if rewards cannot be offered.

- Target 3 may lower self-estimation and render target 4 useless if it involves criticism.
- Target 4, if undertaken in a 'non-structured' manner may depend for success upon the 'personal relationships' between individuals.

We are already aware that although individually identified targets are valid they may be difficult to achieve in isolation. It can now be seen that it would be almost impossible to design a single system which could attack all four target areas simultaneously.

Remember
Different targets need to be met by different means of appraisal, and at different times.

D   *Differing perceptions.* We must always be aware that there may be differing perceptions in regard to the *intention* of performance appraisal systems. If we use 'threatening' terms, any local education authority will need an appraisal system both to maintain organisational control and to improve the efficiency with which human resources, (ie the teachers!) are being used. From the individual teacher's point of view the appraisal system will ideally provide structure within her environment and should also provide feedback from the environment. Whilst it is obviously possible for the LEA and individual expectations and perceptions to coincide, any teacher manager must be aware that there can be a total misfit in both expectation and interpretation.

E   *Changing expectations.* All teachers and teacher managers must recognise this to be the greatest of appraisal danger points, certainly for the next ten-year period. This danger occurs when teachers are working to an agreed appraisal scheme and then the demands on the school change, which effectively changes the teacher's job. When any appraisal system is put into operation it is usually well suited to the needs of the school and the teachers. However, after a period of time, changes of attitude, approaches, role etc, may lead to a mismatch between the system and the school. We must recognise that with the changes required by more major issues such as the Education Reform Act, local management of schools, and local financial management, roles of both schools and individual teachers will be changing rapidly for many years to come.

When the demands on the teachers change and the appraisal system does not, an appraisal system may well deteriorate to the stage where it is only used for 'punishment' or to gain political ends — ie 'deliver the goods'. It can easily be seen that where an appraisal system is allowed to deteriorate it may well 'poison' teachers against any form of appraisal.

Remember

When any appraisal system is used there will be a need to ensure efficient training for all staff involved both to implement and *maintain* any system.

F *How should I approach it?* Teachers should approach the establishment of an appraisal system as a form of *participation*.

WHY?

Because *at its worst* appraisal is a form of behaviour modification which attempts to make a teacher conform to certain ways of working.

Because *at its best* appraisal is something to help and support a teacher, which can make work more satisfying and enjoyable.

In the most supportive of teacher managers and local education authorities any appraisal system will be seen as a form of participation between teacher manager and teacher. It will be seen as part of a process in which there is full and open discussion about targets and the means to attain them. Such a system should also allow all those who wish to be involved in its planning to be able to do so. Participation in appraisal should enable teachers and teacher managers to join together in the search for a continuous development of the skills and abilities of each individual involved.

Remember

Why should I participate in the establishment and maintenance of an appraisal system?

Answer 1 — Appraisal is inevitable, a contractual requirement.
Answer 2 — Participation will make more effective use of all the skills and knowledge available.
Answer 3 — I might get a better deal out of it.
Answer 4 — It is far more pleasant and comfortable than the unpleasant, confrontational approach.

At its best, appraisal should be seen as a process in which teachers, teacher managers and the local education authority influence each other in establishing plans and policies which enable decisions on appraisal to be made.

G   *How does it work? — the starting point.* Appraisal works by *efficiently measuring* the *performance* of the individual teacher or the teacher manager. It does this most efficiently by using a series of stepping stones which the teacher is fully involved in building.

The stepping stones include:

- Agreeing the performance to be measured. In teaching this involves *immediate* as well as short- and long-term goals
- Agreeing the tools to be used to measure the performance.

Remember
A teacher has no basis for appraising herself or judging the quality of progress unless she has stated her aims and set her objectives to achieve them.

Remember
A teacher cannot do this in isolation. She has first to consider the stated aims and objectives of the school in which she works

---

So, where are we?

1 Appraisal goes on all the time.
2 It is done inconsistently.
3 We need a formal system to safeguard and help teachers.
4 Appraisal should improve the quality of teaching and learning.
5 We need from the outset to keep in mind the key dangers and make efforts to avoid them.

2 What are the different methods of appraisal?

In this chapter we are going to suggest that there are four main *approaches* and three key *methods* to consider. We shall also explain why the core of this book is about teacher self-appraisal and indicate an 'appraisal cycle' to help provide a framework for your own personal review.

The four main approaches

A *Comparative procedures*. This approach would compare teacher with teacher against a range of given criteria. The criteria are selected by the management and, in the main, are dimensions which are perceived to be of value to the school as a whole.

Z		Y
✗	punctuality	✓
✗	care with dress	✓
✓	efficient lesson preparation	✗
✓	quiet classes	✓
✗	no playground problems	✓
	BEST TEACHER ➨	✓

B   *Absolute standards.* This approach evaluates the teacher against a set of written standards. Again these standards are set by management, but here the teacher, as an individual, can be judged against several different criteria.

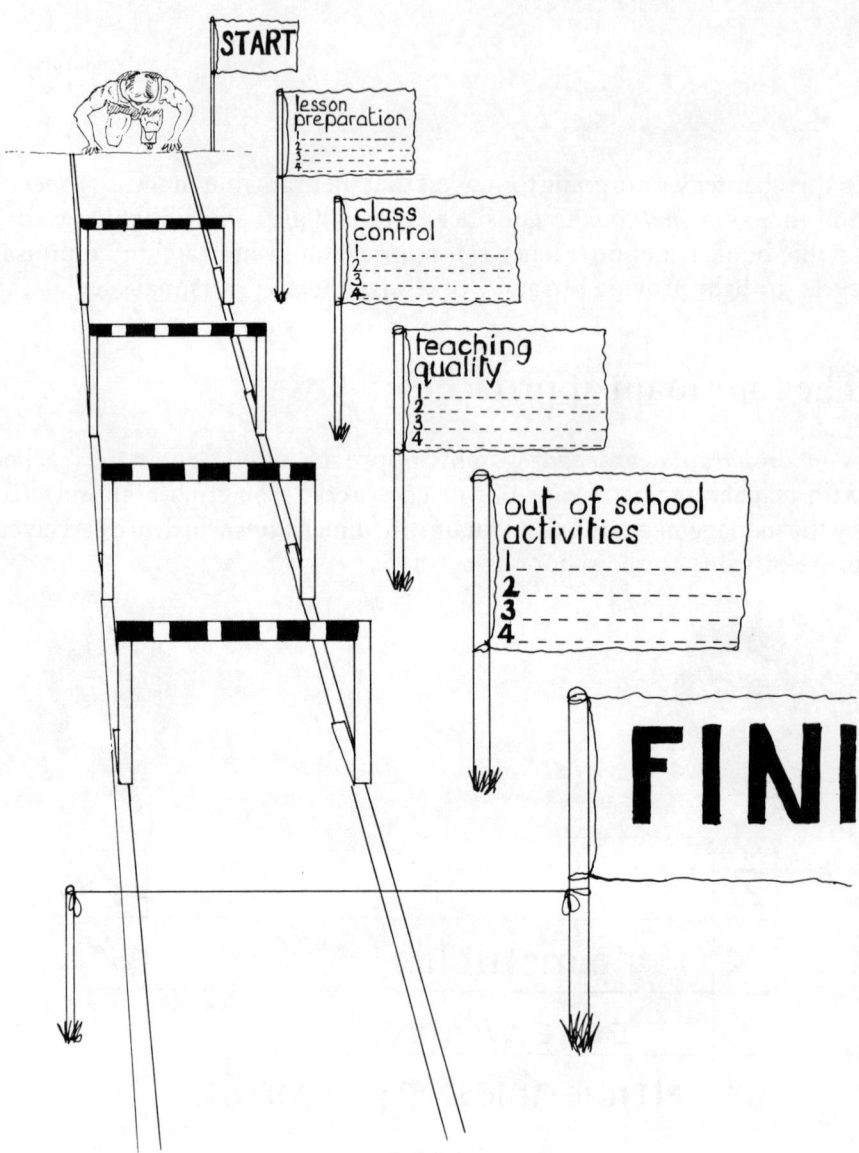

C   *Management by objectives.* In this approach the teacher or the management clearly sets the objectives to be achieved for the individual teacher, and then the teacher is evaluated only in terms of the progress made towards these specifically agreed targets.

Teacher Targets for Summer Term

1. Establish better relationship with Michael.
2. Improve Michael's out of seat behaviour.
3. Complete assessments against English attainment targets.
4. Arrange visits for parents of Joan, Manjit and Winston.
5.

D *Performance indicators*. This approach used to be termed 'direct indexes'. It occurs when targets are laid down for organisational success, and judgements are made purely on the quality of the outcomes.

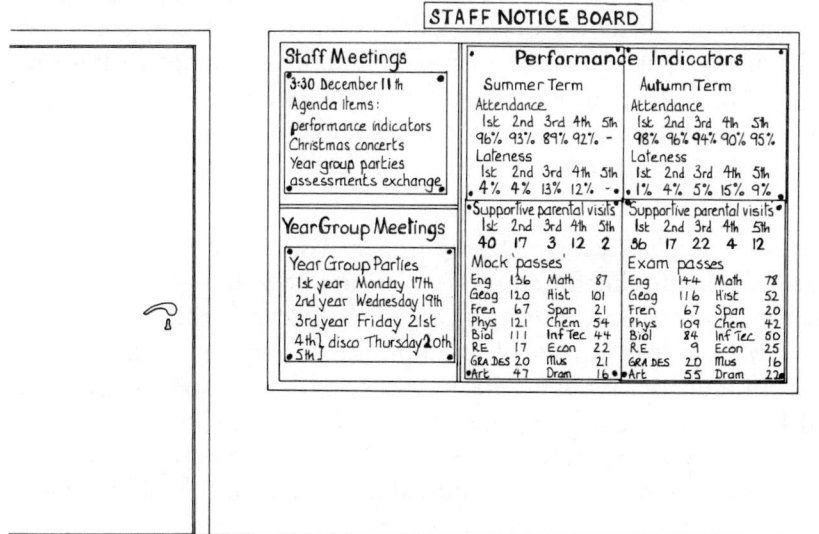

STAFF NOTICE BOARD

Staff Meetings

3·30 December 11th
Agenda Items:
performance indicators
Christmas concerts
Year group parties
assessments exchange

Year Group Meetings

Year Group Parties
1st year Monday 17th
2nd year Wednesday 19th
3rd year Friday 21st
4th disco Thursday 20th
5th

Performance Indicators

Summer Term					Autumn Term				
Attendance					Attendance				
1st	2nd	3rd	4th	5th	1st	2nd	3rd	4th	5th
96%	93%	89%	92%	–	98%	96%	94%	90%	95%
Lateness					Lateness				
1st	2nd	3rd	4th	5th	1st	2nd	3rd	4th	5th
4%	4%	13%	12%	–	1%	4%	5%	15%	9%
Supportive parental visits					Supportive parental visits				
1st	2nd	3rd	4th	5th	1st	2nd	3rd	4th	5th
40	17	3	12	2	36	17	22	4	12

Mock 'passes'

Eng	136	Math	87
Geog	120	Hist	101
Fren	67	Span	21
Phys	121	Chem	54
Biol	111	Inf Tec	44
RE	17	Econ	22
GRA DES	20	Mus	21
Art	47	Dram	16

Exam passes

Eng	144	Math	78
Geog	116	Hist	52
Fren	67	Span	20
Phys	109	Chem	42
Biol	84	Inf Tec	60
RE	9	Econ	25
GRA DES	55	Mus	16
Art	55	Dram	27

The diagram opposite gives an overview of the four approaches, and provides an indication of some of the benefits and dangers involved in each.

Observations in terms of the respective appropriateness of each approach to teacher appraisal are as follows:

1   *Comparative procedures*. The basic aim with regard to this method can appear to be that of maintaining performance at acceptable levels. There would appear to be little to be gained in teaching by making value comparisons between teachers; there are far too many varying items of comparison, from teaching style to class age or social background. It could also be suggested that there is little or no value in assessing a teacher on a global basis. Many ranking items appear inappropriate. Where appraisal provides no practical feedback to the teachers it is of little value.

2   *Absolute standards*. Absolute standards also appear to attempt to maintain performance at acceptable levels, but seem to be far more involved with the identification and improvement of unacceptable behaviour. This appears to be the most dangerous format for teachers. In human developmental terms the approach is crude. Staff could spend a considerable amount of time in assisting with regard to the formulation of items merely to gain a blunt statement of 'fact' in return. The effort made on structuring the item would appear to be in the developmental area, and yet the manager's judgement of standards would tend to be in the personality/characteristics area.

3   *Management by objectives* (MBO). This appears to be firmly based on the concept of enhanced job development and personal growth. Comparisons with others are eradicated, and where the goal-setting is a joint venture it can both prevent subversion of the goal-setting and, without an explicit statement of unacceptability, attempt to improve unacceptable performance. Provided that the overall long-term objectives of the organisation were made explicit and the MBO system could operate within a well-structured framework it would appear to be very well suited for teachers.

4   *Performance indicators*. This approach would not previously have appeared to be suitable for education. We are now, however, having to ensure that performance indicators are identified and utilised. They will have to form at least a part of an appraisal system for evaluating the success or failure of a school. Certainly some of the information gathered would be of value to school management, but not in isolation. Many productivity results in education cannot be appropriately evaluated in terms of the success or failure of individuals. There may be a little more

METHOD	MAJOR FEATURES	PROCEDURES USED	DANGERS	BENEFITS
1 Comparative procedures	1 Evaluation by comparison with other appraisees on dimensions of interest 2 Comparison made on global dimensions of effectiveness to the organisation	1 Straight ranking 2 Alternative ranking 3 Paired comparison 4 Forced distribution	1 Ranking generally made on only one dimension 2 Lack of agreement by appraisers on 'overall' effectiveness 3 Difficult to compare different groups of rankings 4 Little use for feedback or developmental value	1 Free from inter-individual errors 2 Can gain agreement between appraisers
2 Absolute standards	1 Evaluation against written standards 2 Several facets of performance are measured	1 Qualitative methods: — critical incidents — weighted checklist — forced choice 2 Quantitative methods: — conventional rating — behaviourally anchored rating	Inclusion of non-valid items Considerable developmental effort required 1 Easy for assessor to bias assessment 2 Focus on personality characteristics	1 Provide feedback to appraisee 2 Organisation can inform employees of behaviour required by the organisation 3 Employees who are eventually appraised aid in development of forms
3 Management by objectives	1 State clearly the objectives to be accomplished 2 Evaluate progress only in terms of progress towards specifically stated objectives	1 Define employee goals for given time period 2 Employee works to gain established objectives 3 Evaluation of the performance. Emphasis on initial self-appraisal 4 Define new goals for subsequent time period	Difficult to attach rewards equitably Subversion of goal setting	1 Useful developmental tool 2 Can set goals of each individual
4 Performance indicators	1 Measures of productivity 2 Measures of withdrawal	1 Data collection 2 Quality control 1 Absenteeism 2 Turnover	1 Outcomes not clearly definable 2 Outcomes not attributable to the individual 3 Of little value in isolation	1 Not need for appraisal of performance

value in appraising an entire educational organisation on a performance indicator basis, but even so the pitfalls are many and obvious. Performance indicators cannot be the sole approach used to evaluate any individual teacher.

The three major methods

In this section we describe, analyse and compare the three major methods of appraisal:

- self-appraisal
- external appraisal
- group appraisal.

Whilst explaining them we shall make an attempt to identify the strong and weak points of each, and will also attempt to assess the suitability of the methods to different aspects of teaching.

A   *Self-appraisal.* It is fair to say that every individual teacher undertakes some form of self-appraisal on a regular basis. In general terms self-appraisal appears to be good in terms of self-development and the encouragement of personal growth, but can be poor for evaluative purposes. In essence the responsibility is placed upon the individual teacher who must establish short- and long-term performance goals for herself.

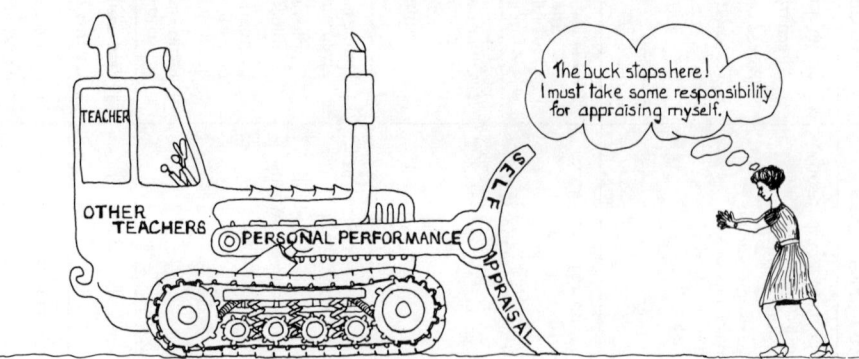

Whatever form of appraisal is considered we would agree strongly with McGregor[2] who suggests that any teacher manager should only be involved in an appraisal system with a teacher after that teacher has:

a) thought a lot about her job;
b) carefully mused on her own strengths and weaknesses;
c) formulated specific plans to accomplish her goals.

Whatever form self-appraisal and self-development takes, it is vital that the individual teacher does not fall into the trap of abdicating her own responsibility for self-development.

> **Remember**
> It is the prime responsibility of any teacher manager to prevent any teacher in his or her care from evading the responsibility of self-development.

B   *External appraisal.* Inherent in the concept of 'external' appraisal is the fact that it is normally performed by teacher managers or external (formally superior) staff. It must be noted that it is not necessarily carried out by one person. It could be argued that it might be far more valid if several teacher managers were involved, they might then tend to observe more of the relevant dimensions of the teacher's behaviour.

In regard to the present applicability of external appraisal, it is interesting to note that it is still most used in education at the interview or selection stage. External appraisal can particularly support the teacher by assisting in the setting of objectives and in providing responsibility for the individual to develop herself. It can provide a good foil by attempting to encourage the teacher to be accountable for her own work. It should attempt to gain the commitment from the teacher which would tempt her away from a possible position of either self-satisfaction or work avoidance, especially where there are tasks which are disliked.

> **Remember**
> External appraisal provides a structured framework which can assist the individual in achieving self-satisfaction. The approach can encourage 'group' involvement and, where successful, the appraisal can directly give the teacher the indications of respect and recognition which she is seeking.

C *Group appraisal.* In group appraisal the assumption is that the appraisal or assessment is a 'team' one with the constant involvement of the individual teacher concerned. Clearly teacher managers and outsiders can be involved in such a process but it must be remembered here that peers and 'subordinates' may also be involved. Group appraisal has many inherent dangers, some of the key ones being:

a) The single greatest danger with *subordinate* appraisal is that the subordinate may make an appraisal based on a personal view, ie how the teacher manager fulfils the individual teacher's needs rather than on her organisational accomplishment.

b) The danger in peer appraisal (as in subordinate appraisal) is that the teacher involved may well lack relevant information and there is a danger of inconsistancy.

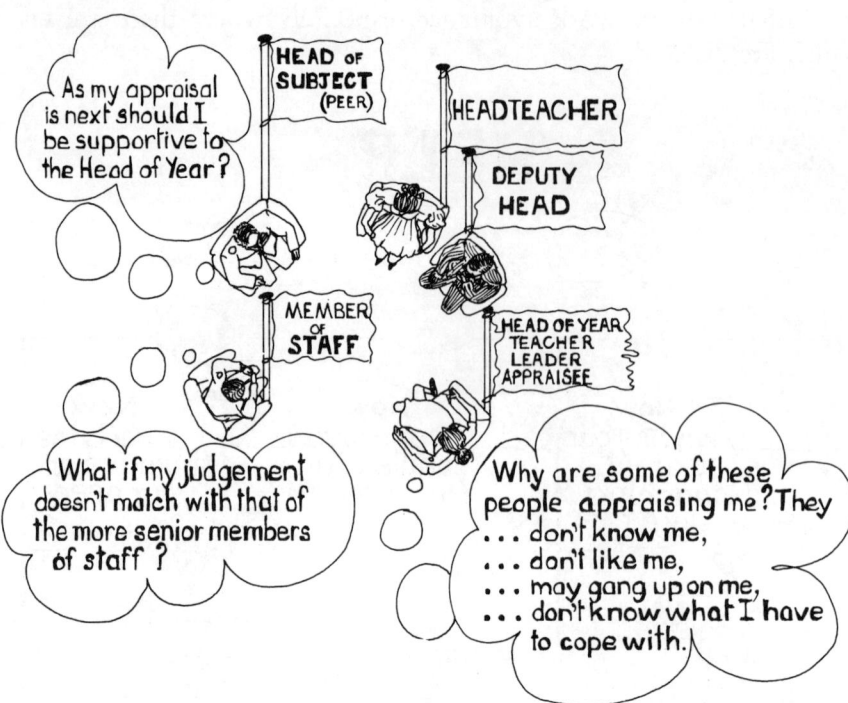

c) In organisational terms group appraisal can be dangerous because, at its worst, it could allow for a lowering of expectations whenever it allows employees (rather than teacher managers) to have a greater influence over other work-force members.

Remember
Group appraisal can encourage staff members to be involved in group situations with peers and subordinates. There are dangers, however, that it could place individual staff in untenable positions and even isolate them from other colleagues.

The diagram overleaf attempts to provide an overview and a clearer comparison between the styles. In summing up the whole issue of different approaches and methods within the diagram the following points must be borne in mind:

1   The major aim for appraisal within education must be to become both developmental and supportive. We need to aim, at the outset, to build relationships, cut down stress and engender feelings of competence. We must be aware, therefore, that at different times and in different settings, different appraisal systems *will* be appropriate.

2   We need to be aware of, and counter, the strong argument within education which states that because of the wide range of possible negative outcomes appraisal should only be used for development and not for evaluation.

3   We need, therefore, to enhance job development and personal growth whilst not dodging the issue that we need to identify and improve unacceptable performance.

4   Industrial and organisational appraisal has traditionally been carried out by an employee's immediate superior. This has not been so in education where, in a range of forms, it has tended to have been carried out by the headteacher. It is true to say that the headteacher (with the governors) is in a position to reward and punish teachers, but the Head can tend to be well removed from any objective evaluation.

5   The single greatest appraisal problem for education is that of alienating people in a job where they work with other human beings. Any negative effects of an appraisal system may destroy relationships between teacher and pupil and be far more harmful than in industry.

6   For a long period in education the responsibility for appraisal has been left with the individual concerned, often with little or no support to undertake it appropriately. This has now become unacceptable, not

SYSTEM STYLES	JUSTIFICATION	FOCUS	PROBLEMS	APPLICABILITY
Self-appraisal	Good where performer is in best position to observe and evaluate her own methods of work and outcome.	Provides developmental focus for performance evaluation. Emphasis is on personal growth, self-motivation and organisational potential of employee. Provides self-feedback.	1 Low agreement between self- and supervisory appraisals. Subordinates tend to evaluate their performance more favourably than do superiors.	1 Isolated performers, eg specialist units. 2 Unique possessors of rare skill, eg computers in special education.
External appraisal a by superiors	1 Hierarchy of formal authority legitimates the right of the superior to evaluate. 2 Manager normally controls the rewards and punishment system.	1 It is the duty and obligation of the manager to evaluate her staff. 2 Improvement of performance. 3 Tie in performance to rewards.	1 Can be a threat to employee, especially where tied to rewards and punishment. 2 Often one-way flow of information from superior to inferior, it places inferior in justification role. 3 Appraiser often feels uncomfortable, may not have the skills needed to appraise.	Any formal organisation.
b by outsiders	1 Need for specialised expertise. 2 Objectivity of appraisal can be ensured by someone without a vested interest in the outcome.	Specialised trained observer in a specific content area.	1 Can be interpreted as manager 'getting rid' of distasteful chore. 2 Acceptance by workforce of the outsiders 'knowledge' or expertise. 3 Time element involved.	1 Arbitration situations. 2 Interview/appointment situations.

Group appraisal a Peers	1 Reduction of threat with regard to status differentials. 2 Production of a non-competitive system. 3 Peers have more information about each other than do superiors.	1 More accurate observations of behaviour. 2 Communication and co-ordination of problems between working group.	1 Value depreciated by competitive nature of rewards. 2 Personal friendship bias. 3 Whom do I select to assess me?	1 Senior management situations — Headteachers. 2 Teachers developing appraisal skills.
b Subordinates	1 Power equalisation. 2 Modification of superiors' behaviour.	1 Gain subordinates' perceptions of superior.	1 Subordinates may perceive it as illegitimate. 2 Potentially stressful for subordinate — 'the threat' of an honest appraisal. 3 Superiors view it with suspicion. 4 Can undermine legitimate positional power.	Normally considered unacceptable.

only because of the formal requirement for an appraisal system but also because of the rapidly changing nature of the education system which now involves a National Curriculum, local financial management, programmes of study, attainment targets, assessment procedures and performance indicators — to name but a few!

7   When starting to initiate an appraisal system any teacher manager will need to take into account the self-motivating nature of human beings, and will need to accept that the general response of the work-force will initially be on the negative side in its commitment to any appraisal system.

8   Teacher managers must recognize that appraisal systems may flounder if they are not soundly designed with a clear set of purposes in mind, and if they are not structured to meet the needs of the individual organisation concerned.

9   There is no single appropriate approach to performance appraisal. Different appraisal approaches should be matched to the specific organisational needs. Several approaches may be used at different times within a single organisation.

10   Every teacher manager needs to understand and *remove* the perceived threats and stress of an appraisal scheme to the work-force.

Remember
Whatever system is selected it will only be *successful* if:

a) within a school system of appraisal each individual teacher is willing conscientiously to undertake continuous self-appraisal;
b) within an Authority's system of appraisal each individual school is willing conscientiously to undertake continual self-appraisal.

Remember
The authors are strong believers in performance appraisal and are convinced that there is an essential need for appraisal systems within schools. They do not attempt to dodge the key issue of the need for appraisal systems but also feel it is a great danger area for education, with many pitfalls. They attempt to suggest that progress should be made, but with caution and sensitivity. They believe that a key to development is self-appraisal for teachers, with teachers themselves gaining confidence in handling many of the evaluative tools available.

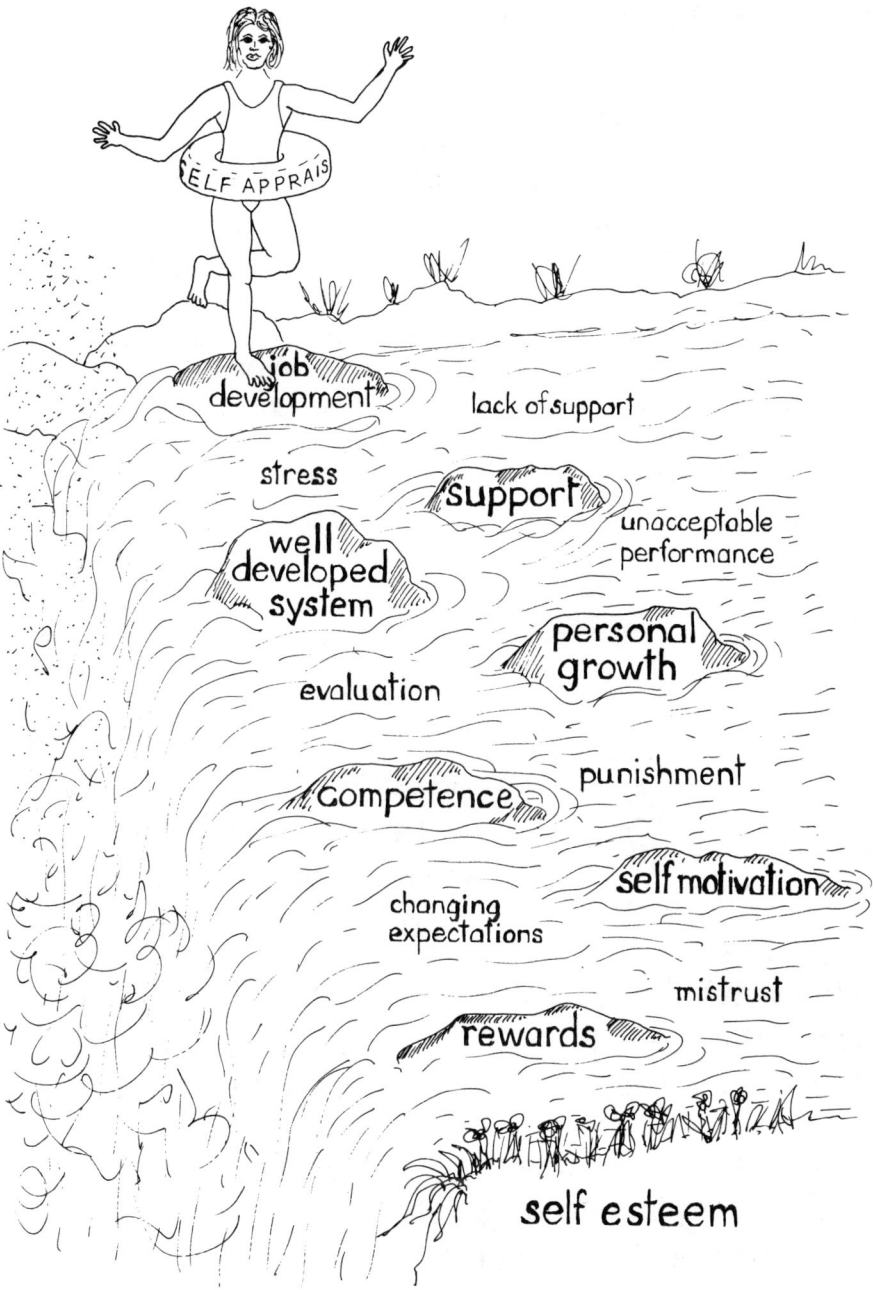

The appraisal stepping stones

Self-evaluation — the key

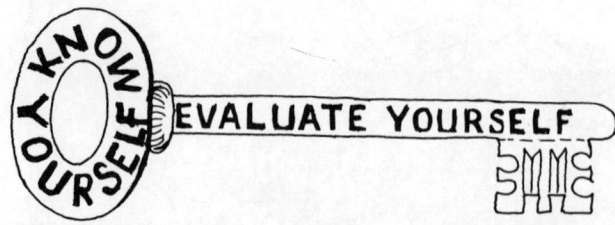

A statement has been made indicating that whatever system of appraisal is selected or, in the case of the DES, imposed, it will only be successful where teachers give commitment to, and have expertise in, the area of self-evaluation. Perhaps the best definition of a *successful* appraisal system should be:

● a system which gets support from the appraiser and appraised.

I like this.
I'm getting time, attention,
support and interest
is being paid to me.
I feel I'm improving
as a teacher.

I like this.
I know what I'm doing.
The setting is right.
The structure is
      available.
The time is available.
I'm getting to know the
member of staff involved.

There is little doubt that many teachers and many schools accept that self-evaluation is an integral part of their work and they are constantly reviewing their activities and assessing their levels of performance.

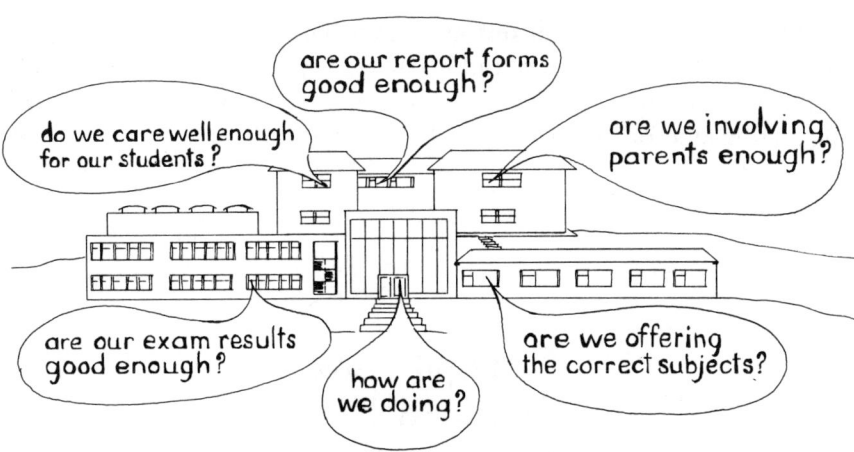

The terms of reference for this book were to produce a framework, some guidelines, and a series of practical tools to assist teachers to enhance their skills in self-evaluation. The book also suggests that it would be both helpful and appropriate for individual teachers to work together at times with a colleague. This would enable them to share the development of self-evaluation skills and also to moderate and cross-check each other's performance.

Some principles for self-evaluation:

A   *Accountability.* The undertaking of self-appraisal enables the teacher to become both more accountable to herself and to the learners she works with. It also enables teachers to judge whether they are prepared to take the necessary steps to develop.

B   *Self-criticism.* Have you seriously considered the outcomes of your work in regard to colleagues and learners? The greatest danger in self-evaluation is complacency. It is for this reason that it will help to work with a colleague on occasions, and to talk to others about your self-evaluation.

C   *The 'model' teacher.* By working on appraisal it may easily be considered that there is a model of the ideal teacher in mind. This should not be the case, but two things should be kept in mind:

- there should be a minimal level of functioning within all basic skills areas which are required to do any particular job
- testing yourself against good practice elsewhere is a vital part of self-development and appraisal.

Remember
However the individual teacher goes about self-evaluation, she should always have two key questions in mind:

- what aspects of current performance do I need to improve?
- what new skills do I need to equip myself with, and what new knowledge do I need, whether for improvement in my present post or for a future move?

D   *Structure.* Although we are talking about the teacher appraising herself, it is vital for the individual concerned to be self-prepared and appropriately structured before starting. The teacher needs to be clear about the exercise being undertaken and should have simply recorded the structures to be effected. Simple items should be covered such as:

- what aspects of the work should be evaluated?
- in what order of priority should they be evaluated?
- what tools should be used to evaluate them (see chapter 4)?
- what timescale should be chosen?
- how should the exercise be recorded?
- will support or resources be required, from reference materials or other colleagues?

The diagram overleaf provides a simple framework for undertaking self-evaluation. It must be remembered that the evaluation can be of a particular aspect of work over a relatively short timescale at the outset, whilst skills are built up. It must also be remembered that a teacher's own objectives *must* be in accord with the overall context of the school setting.

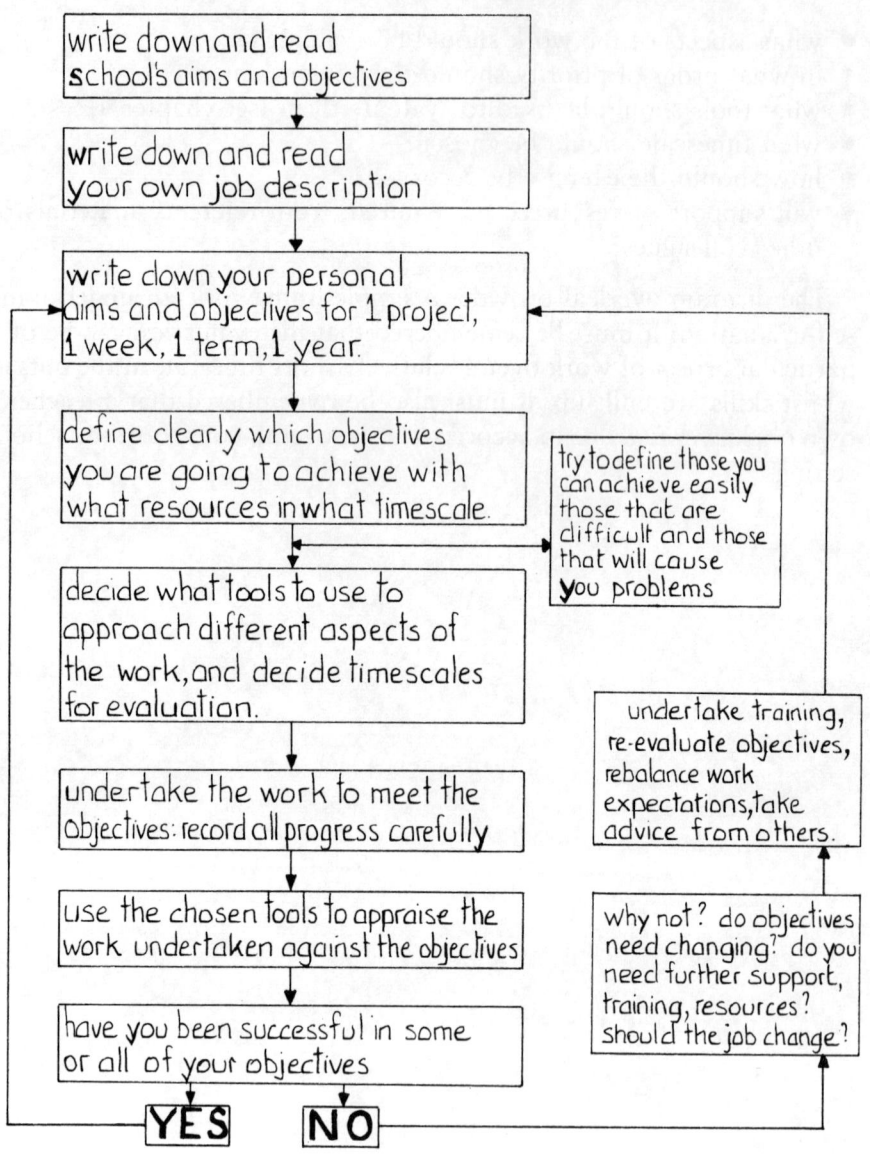

A Self-Appraisal Cycle

write down and read school's aims and objectives

write down and read your own job description

write down your personal aims and objectives for 1 project, 1 week, 1 term, 1 year.

define clearly which objectives you are going to achieve with what resources in what timescale.

try to define those you can achieve easily those that are difficult and those that will cause you problems

decide what tools to use to approach different aspects of the work, and decide timescales for evaluation.

undertake the work to meet the objectives: record all progress carefully

undertake training, re-evaluate objectives, rebalance work expectations, take advice from others.

use the chosen tools to appraise the work undertaken against the objectives

have you been successful in some or all of your objectives

why not? do objectives need changing? do you need further support, training, resources? should the job change?

YES   NO

3 How do I talk about my performance?

One of the most difficult things for any professional person to be able to do is to talk about his or her work within an appraisal setting. Teachers should be encouraged, at the earliest stage, to build up the skills to do this successfully. It is a helpful and natural development from self-appraisal to involve a colleague in the aspects of appraisal and then to undertake some discussions on the observations and outcomes.

Remember
Teachers can only talk about their performance within an appraisal setting, either with other teachers or teacher managers, with *good preparation* by both.

The following series of notes and sketches will offer a structure for talking about performance, and will indicate some of the vital skills that each teacher and teacher manager needs to develop. The structure is just as relevant where:

- a teacher is talking about her performance with a colleague teacher
- a teacher is talking to a teacher manager (or vice versa).

Remember
You are likely to be in *both* positions at different times, both appraising and being appraised.

Whenever possible, work with a colleague on an aspect of appraisal and then take the opportunity to rehearse the roles of teacher *and* teacher manager whilst undertaking an appraisal dialogue. Be willing from the outset to learn to accept criticisms, observations and advice.

Our sketches cover the following aspects of the appraisal dialogue:

The Appraisal Dialogue — What is it?

Should be :

formal in approach
informal in nature
two-way discussion
frank and honest
individual
on a regular basis
confidential
supportive
developmental

Should be about:

raising issues of concern
defining the help needed
planning for the future
a review of the work done
on improving performance

The Appraisal Dialogue
Questions in the mind

am I running my school/department
   efficiently?
am I communicating well?
are we clear about our joint objectives?
am I supporting my staff appropriately?
does this person
need further
training?

do we
   have mutual
      understanding?

does anyone
   out there know about me?
   how am I doing?
      how do you regard me?
   where do I go from here?
what exactly is my job?

The Appraisal Dialogue
Preparation – What's in the mind/
planning of the appraiser

I must check the job description.
I must read my file which includes
details of all our previous meetings
(formal and informal) and visits to classrooms
with the teacher.
I must remind myself of the targets set.
I must remind myself of the teacher's
strengths and weaknesses.

I look forward to seeing you
and will give you at least one
week's notice.
Let's remind each other of the
purpose and exactly what we
will cover.
Please think back over the last __ months
on all aspects that we shall be covering.
Do suggest where you think further
training will be needed.
Do think how your strengths will be needed.
Do consider whether I have helped to
achieve your goals or not.

The Appraisal Dialogue

The Interview Arrangements

allow sufficient time
- minimum of 1 hour

use an appropriate room
- with appropriate furniture

ensure no interruptions
- engaged sign on door
- phone off the hook

create a calm atmosphere
- quiet, comfortable

be consistent
- same type of arrangements for everyone

The Appraisal Dialogue
During the Interview

What should I, as a teacher, <u>expect</u> to occur during the interview.

* praise for good work done
* constructive criticism for mistakes or problem issues
* advice over teaching methods
* an opportunity for counselling on personal issues
* guidance on in-service training policy
* evidence that the manager has prepared well for our talk and knows me
* detailed analysis of my work
* guidance on reading
* help to prepare a training or support programme for me
* advice on school organisation and management issues

The Appraisal Dialogue
The End of the Interview

Did I cover all aspects of the teacher's work?
Did we agree on the levels of functioning?
Did we talk about the balance of work and interrelation between parts?
Did I leave the teacher with a clear view of how he is regarded?
Did we agree objectives to be achieved for the next appraisal?
Have I a clear view of the support needed?
If I write down what I now feel will it come as a surprise to the teacher?

Did I enjoy that review?
Was it helpful to me?
Do I feel motivated to further development?
Can I look forward positively to the next appraisal meeting?

The Appraisal Dialogue
Recording the Outcome

Talking is of little value without an accurate record.
When undertaking an appraisal dialogue it is vital
to take notes of the discussion and also vital
to write up the notes into a <u>record</u> of the
appraisal, immediately afterwards.

I've written up
the notes of our meeting
as quickly as I could. I've
built them upon the notes I
took during our meeting.
Would you like to read them
and let me know if they
accurately reflect all
that was said.

It will make a change
to have something in
writing.
I'm glad there are
going to be no more
hidden records.

Thanks, I'll do that.
It will be helpful to
have an accurate
record. It can provide
the starting point
for our next
discussion.

The Appraisal Dialogue

Preparing for the next session

Could I have handled that any differently?
Are you happy about the way we are working together?
Did you find the records helpful?
Are you clear what has to be done by the time we meet next?
We can meet at agreed time intervals or sooner if either of us feels it will help.

It's nice to be asked how I felt about it.
Its nice to know I have someone to go to for support who knows what I'm trying to do.
I'd better be well prepared for my next session.

How often do we meet?
Can we meet sooner if I reach my targets or need support?

The Appraisal Dialogue
The Developing Relationship

We are jointly working out how I am/she is doing.
We are jointly trying to work out what causes
success and failure for me and her.
We are jointly setting appropriate objectives for
my work and her work.
We are jointly setting realistic timescales for
my work and her work.
We are jointly trying to build on a base
of success.
<u>We are jointly responsible for
my work and her work</u>

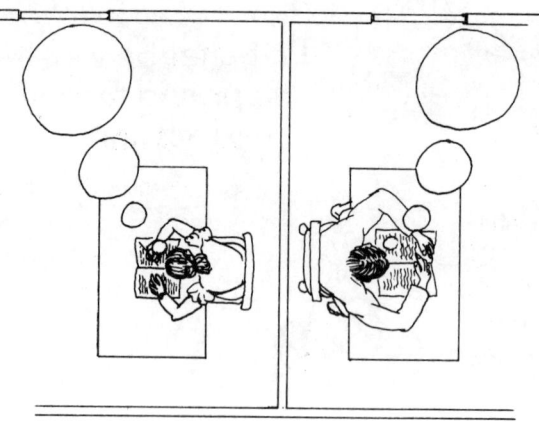

4 What do I need to consider when appraising myself as a teacher?

Introduction

In this chapter we suggest that there are four key things to consider when appraising your performance as a teacher.

First there is the need to recognise that you carry out your functions in a range of contexts and, although it is of primary importance that you are effective in your classroom delivery, it is also important that you contribute positively in all other contexts.

Second the role of a teacher is multi-faceted and in the different contexts referred to above there are many separate aspects, each of which needs to be considered when reflecting on your performance.

Third the process of self-appraisal must be structured and systematic if it is to be effective. We offer you a set of guidelines which you will need to apply if you are to gain an accurate and realistic view of your work.

Finally we draw attention to factors which may get in the way of your effective performance. These factors are not offered as sources of potential excuse for under-achievement, but in coming to a view of your performance, you should attempt to see it in the light of the situation in which you are working. If you work in this systematic way you will enhance your classroom performance through gaining a clearer vision of what works well with your pupils and why other things do not work so well and therefore require attention. This process will automatically lead to a clarification of your professional development needs and prepare you for the formal process of professional appraisal by providing clear insights into your personal strengths, limitations and needs.

The contexts in which I work

During each working day all teachers are exposed to a variety of different situations, each of which requires involvement and, therefore, provides a basis for reviewing personal effectiveness. The list below could well come from the start of a normal school day for most teachers.

Preparing to leave home	— gather together all materials to be taken to school today.
Arriving at school	— take materials to classroom; clean blackboard ready for first lesson; check arrangements for afternoon with Mr X; remember to remind Miss Y about pupil Z; remember to arrange meeting with headteacher.
Going to staff room	— check today's notices; spend brief time socially with colleagues; collect personal post; look for Miss Y, write note and put in pigeon hole.
Going to school office	— gain attention of busy secretary; check availability of head for meeting; leave clear message for head requesting meeting; reassure secretary of need for meeting; collect class register
Going to classroom	— prepare mentally to receive class; check notices to be given out; welcome class members on arrival; check that pupil Z is present; settle class for registration; register class; give out notices; ask class for their notices to each other; settle class for first lesson; have word with pupil Z about Miss Y's need to see her.

The above list does not include any formal teaching, but even at this stage the teacher has operated a range of management and organisational skills and used considerable knowledge and experience. For most teachers this level of performance is part of their 'normal', almost subconscious daily routine. As with the experienced, effective driver who goes from A to B without conscious thought, and is occasionally shocked on arrival by her lack of awareness of the journey, so too the experienced, effective teacher succeeds without knowing always how the success was gained. This could well be true for all aspects of a teacher's

The classroom context

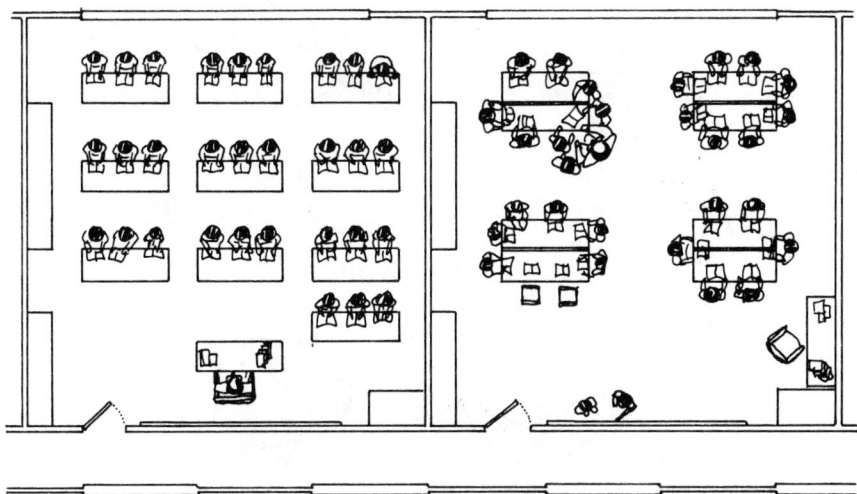

work and the aim of this section is to increase awareness of the range of contexts in which most teachers fulfil their role.

This is the major location for the formal expression of a teacher's purpose — ie teaching. It is not necessarily the major location for some pupils' learning, and all teachers should be aware of other forms of pupil learning which can be drawn into classroom teaching. In particular, in early years education, the initial learning experiences in the home underpin the main potential for success at school.

Aspects for consideration. In the classroom the teacher mainly (possibly always) functions as the sole adult in this setting. Here she is responsible for formal and informal controls and interactions; access to new knowledge, skills and experience; and monitoring and assessing each learner's performance.

In this context the teacher is also a manager; a manager of resources; a manager of individuals, groups and the whole class; a manager of learning experiences; and is, therefore, responsible and accountable for the quality of all that occurs within this context.

The staff group

This is one major location for direct professional support and affirmation. It is a base for checking meanings, gaining greater understanding; a forum for expressing reservations, and a source of opportunity for seeking and gaining support.

The 'health' of this setting is crucial to the well-being of the individuals within it. When the health is positive it frees individuals to test

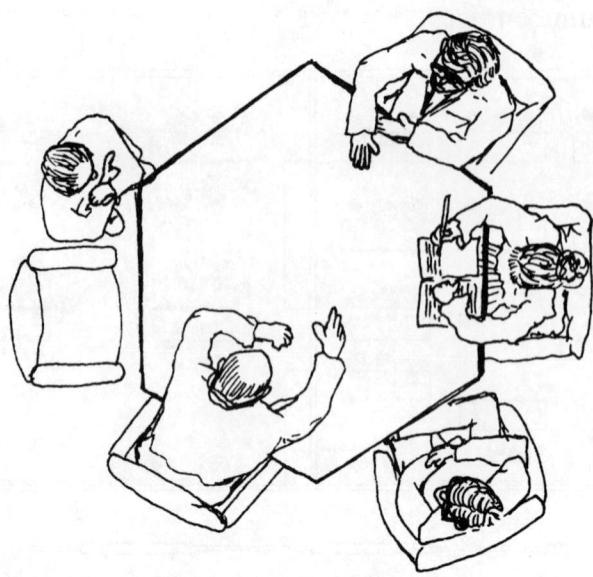

ideas, to risk errors and to grow greater personal confidence. The resulting corporate spirit both feeds the quality of interpersonal skill development and underpins much of the quality of classroom practice.

Teachers may be members of different formal groups in schools. In secondary schools these could be departmental groups, year groups and task groups set up for specific purposes. It is not unusual under these circumstances for senior staff to function as group members under the leadership of individuals at lower levels of overall responsibility, introducing the need to give and take leadership in different settings.

In primary schools the groupings are more often related to year group or curriculum-specific working groups. In small primary schools all teachers may be members of all groups with individuals taking different roles in different settings. The individual teacher is mainly responsible for functioning as group or team member and contributes ideas, information, personal experience, reactions, suggestions etc. The quality of a teacher's listening skills, questioning, analysis and positive intervention is important in this setting.

In this context the teacher may also be a manager and, therefore, carry responsibility and accountability for the quality of the group's work.

The staffroom

This is often the focal point for much of the formal and informal organisational and managerial work of the staff; the 'alternative seat of government' of those with informal authority born of their skill, wit, experience or personal power. The staffroom is a major centre for

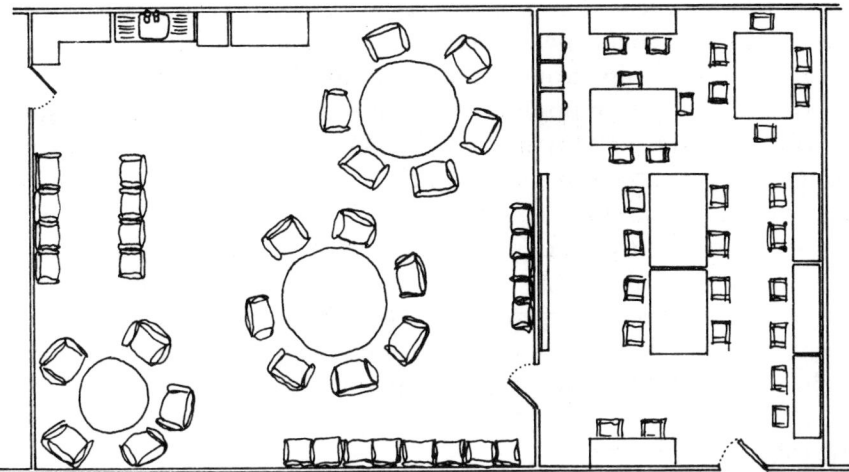

information exchange, and bargaining for support and assistance; a haven for those whose classroom experience is a source of stress; a platform for those whose opinions others will have to hear; a challenge for those whose interpersonal skills are not yet up to the task, and a threat for those who are at odds with their peers.

In this context the qualities of the person are at least as important as the skills of the teacher. Forming and maintaining a range of relationships within the staff group binds together the adult community and helps to provide a wider range of other learning opportunities for pupils through the self-supported enterprise of staff initiative and the capacity of the teachers to respond positively to the needs of pupils in their care.

Social settings

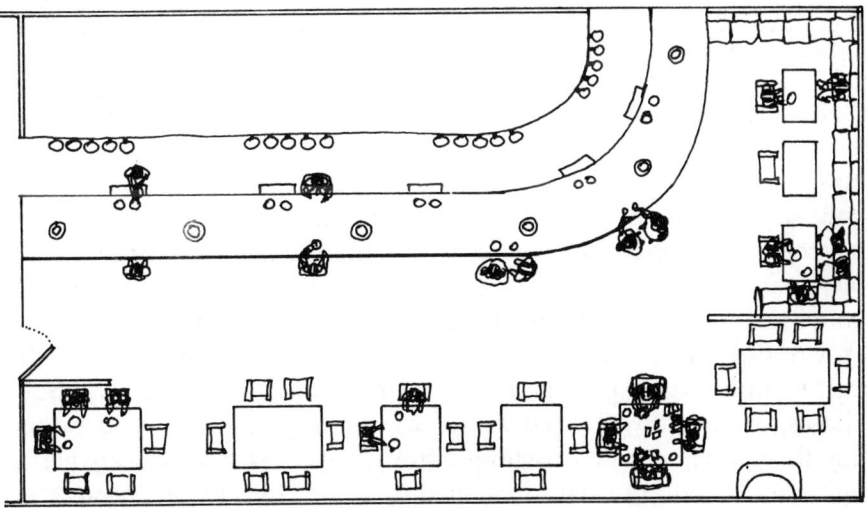

The social life of teaching staff often extends beyond the school and the time that the teachers spend there. Most frequently this contact is restricted to friendship groups, though it may have a wider basis for support through common interests in sport or other activities. In some schools the social life is maintained as an ordered and well-managed formal social structure of events which draw in other friends and members of teachers' families. It is not uncommon in secondary schools for the social settings to include pupils, especially if the schools have a sixth form, and where this is organised in ways which still maintain necessary distinctions between teachers and taught, it adds significantly to the overall quality of the school as a learning community. In this context teachers' personal qualities are paramount.

The local community

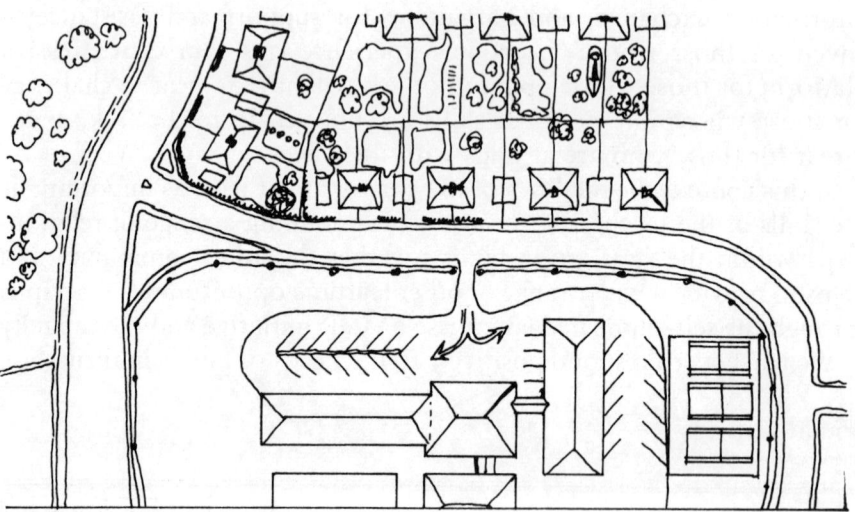

This context is probably the most varied from school to school; especially those with reception classes and/or nursery units. The scope for links with the home is enormous and a vital component of the success of the school. Developing the confidence of parents is essential expecially if, through the first child, they may be re-entering the world of education for the first time. In schools which service bi-lingual learners both pre-school and home-school links are crucial, and the parent may represent a key resource in assisting early learning in the mother tongue. Sadly the positive links with home and the community, so often seen in infant schools, are not always maintained as pupils grow older, and by the time they enter secondary school many of their parents feel unable to visit school, and are even threatened by the prospect. This is not true when schools foster close community links so that adults in the local community see the school as their environment as well as that of their children, and for this to succeed teachers need to adopt a policy of more open access for parents.

In this context the teacher needs a range of skills beyond those employed at formal parents' evenings which merely keep parents informed of their children's progress. The teacher needs a wider range of communication skills and an ability to empathise with the parents, seeing their needs and their situation as the priority for their attention. Listening skills, patience and an ability to maintain composure in the face of demanding circumstances are important aspects of the teacher's role in this context.

The headteacher and senior management team

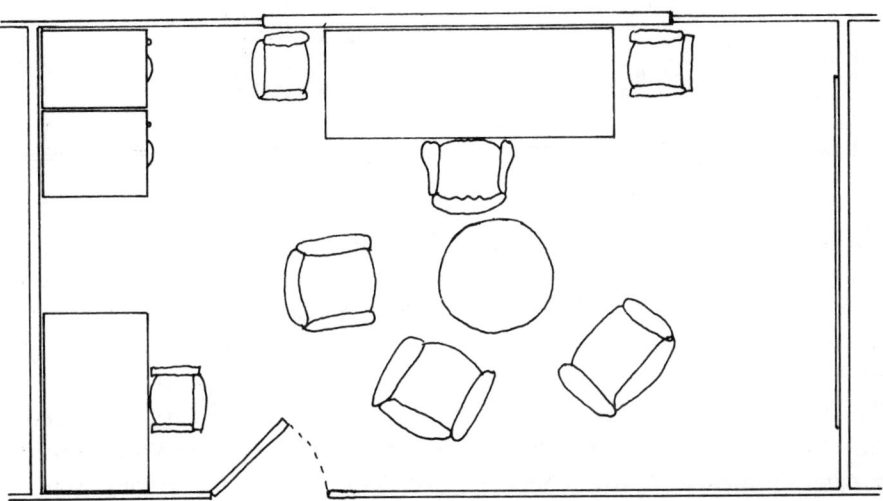

The headteacher and senior management team are responsible for most of the decision-making that controls the ultimate quality of the teaching and learning in a school. They lead in managing the curriculum; the learning resources; the use of time; the allocation of finance; the collection of evidence of performance; all communication between the school and the outside world; and the overall quality of the learning environment and its ethos and culture. In this context teachers' access to involvement and participation may lie outside their personal control and, in the absence of an appropriate appraisal system, it may not be founded on adequate objective indicators of potential for further responsibility. Especially as, under the current legislation concerning the governance of schools, the authority, accountability and responsibility of the headteacher has been significantly increased including responsibility for staff development. In this situation the teacher requires clarity in the presentation of ideas and aspirations.

The governing body

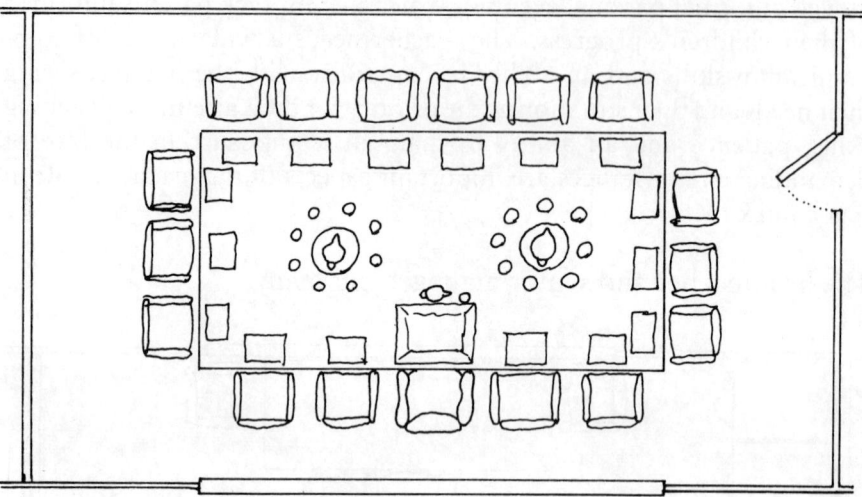

Until the passing of the Education Reform Bill most teachers experienced little contact with the governors of their school. This is likely to change drastically, especially in those schools where the governors have the confidence and interest to fulfil their responsibilities directly, including oversight of the curriculum, its implementation and evaluation. Through teacher-governors the staff can expect to be kept informed, but there has been a major shift in power, and the governors have much greater influence than in the past, especially over staff appointments, promotions and dismissals.

   In this context it is essential that teachers are in a position to describe their own performance based upon an accurate and objective collection of evidence.

Personal and career development

The notion that teachers are trained once for the forty years that they work has never been acceptable. Such is the current pace of change in education that it is now impossible for any teacher to function effectively without keeping abreast of new developments and extending her knowledge, experience and skills.

   In this context it is important that teachers maintain their reading of educational publications and take advantage of the in-service training opportunities on offer to them. Whilst this poses a great challenge to

teachers it also provides great opportunities for career development. New tasks and new structures will always open up space for forward-thinking, well-prepared and hard-working individuals. The free market economy imposed by current legislation brings no threat to the competent teacher.

Summary

The effective teacher works well in a range of contexts. She is a good classroom teacher; plays a part in the work of the teacher groups to which she belongs; contributes to the general life of the school and the social and professional life of the staff; represents the school well in its relationship with the local community it serves; is aware of the overall policies of the senior management team and the aspirations of the governors; is in touch with developments in education and is working to develop her skills and knowledge, thereby widening her range of experience.

The different aspects of teaching against which self-appraisal can be applied

The role of teacher is multi-faceted, and when collecting information about your performance you should focus on specifically defined aspects of your work in order to gain maximum clarity of insight into its quality. In this section we have listed many aspects of teaching to assist you in identifying your points of key focus. Our assumption is that the effective teacher is functioning well in all aspects of her work though we recognise and accept that the level of effectiveness varies from aspect to aspect and, over time, in relation to the different contexts in which teachers teach.

Use the following lists as check lists both for identifying and recording points for attention.

Pupils

Knowledge of their names; relationships; abilities — limitations and potential; past experience; family — siblings; medical information.

Developed 'image' of each pupil.

Staff relationships

Knowledge of formal staffing structure; formal authority structure; informal authority structure; line management arrangements; basic expectations re dress, punctuality, form of address etc; social structure and participation; groupings and territorial space;

Management

Quality of lesson preparation; forward planning; allocation of tasks and roles; implementation of decisions for action; identified needs for action; analysis of situations; relationships with others — establishing new and maintaining old; recorded information and its storage/retrieval.

School's management team

Knowledge of the different role and responsibilities of the various members of the management team.

Knowledge of the day-to-day duties of senior management team members in relation to expectations of staff, eg cover arrangements for staff absence; access to resources for in-service training; access to curriculum-development funds; access to staff working groups and committees; access to general information.

Knowledge of timetabling arrangements and future curriculum planning.

Governors

Knowledge of membership, especially teacher representatives and parent representatives.

Access to records of past meetings and agendas of future meetings.

Awareness of mechanism for getting views expressed through teacher members; governors' key policy objectives for the school's future; the information requirements on governing bodies for parents.

Access to informal contact in social settings to increase personal awareness.

LEA

Knowledge of advisory and support services; in-service training; education officers — personnel and finance; addresses and telephone numbers of key people; LEA budget and school's allocated budget; appointments procedures; employment-related information — codes of practice; elected members and committee structure.

DES

Knowledge of role and structure of HMI; recent documentation — circulars and Acts; timetables for implementation of national initiatives; specific grants.

School culture

Knowledge of rules, regulations and guidelines; acceptable behaviour — pupil and teacher; social life of school; recreational opportunities; parental involvement in and penetration of the systems; trade union activity/expectations; peer group norms; quality of environment; interaction between teaching and non-teaching staff.

Parents

Knowledge of home addresses, telephone numbers and circumstances; known expectations for children at school level of active involvement in school; linguistic diversity/mother tongue.

Quality of reporting to parents on pupils' performance.

Confidence in meeting and coping with parents.

Community

Knowledge of ethnic diversity of intake; religious diversity of intake; special festivals and celebrations; aspirations and expectations for development; links between school and the local community, and with local business and industry; socially disadvantaged areas.

Professional skills and knowledge

Ability to design and produce good-quality learning resources; manage classroom-learning resources; display work effectively; continuously assess pupils' work and progress.

Quality of personal recording; personal reporting; class groupwork; resource-based learning; behavioural control and management.

Ability to articulate a point of view with clarity; debate and discuss whilst maintaining a personal agenda; work in problem-solving situations; work well with others; use personal time effectively; prioritise actions under stress.

Knowledge of assessment and diagnostic techniques; recording techniques — databases etc; reporting rechniques; learning theory, language development theory and classroom management theory.

Basic guidelines for self-appraisal

Self-appraisal is an essential part of the effective teacher's normal way of working. The process of reflecting on performance: definition of objectives; analysis of outcomes; checking outcomes with objectives; re-thinking content and method of approach; and talking about teaching and learning with teachers and pupils, makes for better performance.

But if this process is to fulfil its true potential it has to be carried out in a structured and organised fashion. The list below represents the basic rules to be followed:

1 Do not use a single sample.
2 Always review against pre-stated objectives expressed as personal targets and/or intended learning outcomes.
3 Agree your criteria for effectiveness before reflecting on your work.
4 Whenever possible involve another teacher in the process.
5 Allow adequate time for preparation, collecting your evidence, analysing your evidence and discussing each of these stages with a trusted, experienced colleague.
6 Always be fair with yourself and keep things in perspective.
7 Find a way of making your self-knowledge explicit.
8 Do not put too much pressure on yourself — focus on one or two aspects of your work that need attention.
9 Use appropriate tools to collect your evidence.
10 Be honest with yourself.
11 Whenever possible tie in your self-appraisal to your school's organisational appraisal.

1 Do not use a single sample

For obvious reasons collecting evidence from only one class of pupils is inadequate. All teachers perform at different levels of effectiveness according to the age and ability of their pupils and the content and process of their required teaching. The most gifted teacher with a record of Oxbridge successes from 'A' level classes may live in fear of weekly encounters with younger or less-motivated pupils. The gifted developer of early language and number skills in your children may purposefully avoid essential work in science or music with the same group of pupils because she feels incompetent in these areas.

Within the working week virtually all teachers pass up and down the continuum which has at one end complete, relaxed competence and enjoyment, whilst at the other it has insecurity, stress and unhappiness. Of course some teachers find that they have skills for working with pupils of certain aptitude and ability and lack the necessary repertoire to move easily outside this range. Whilst this may be true it hardly represents a reasonable basis for career development, nor does it allow for effective management of staff resources. For both reasons it is essential that teachers work to broaden their range of experiences and skills and start by collecting evidence of the quality of their work from a range of classes or curriculum situations.

Task

List all the classes you teach, or if you work with just one class, list the curriculum areas you cover in one week. Make a note of the times during the week that you spend with the classes or on the listed curriculum activities. Consider each session in terms of difficulties you experience or the success you are having. Score each in the boxes provided from 1–10, ie 1 = least difficulty or least success, 10 = greatest difficulty or greatest success.

We suggest that you carry out your initial self-appraisal using three differing groups and/or sessions to give you a spread of experience,

Teaching group or curriculum area	Contact sessions during the week	Difficulty	Success	Chosen group and session

preferably avoiding the extremes. Identify your three chosen groups in the right-hand column.

2 Always review against pre-stated objectives expressed as personal targets and/or intended learning outcomes

If this seems like going back to teaching practice then that's exactly what it is. Only by stating clear aims and objectives can you make any valid judgement about the quality of your work and the general direction of your development. Aims and objectives can be described in terms of personal aims and pupil responses. You will need to separate these out in your planning and implementation stages in order to be clear on the outcomes.

Some examples of personal aims might be:

- To make more effective use of time in my lessons
- To involve my pupils more actively in my lessons
- To give greater support to bilingual learners in my class
- To make better use of audio-visual material in my teaching
- To improve the quality of group work in my classes
- To gain class control more readily at the start of lessons
- To use more open questioning in class discussion
- To talk less and get the pupils to talk more.

The example below illustrates objectives to achieve one of the aims in more detail.

To gain class control more readily at the start of lessons:

- arrive in class before the first pupil
- have all materials organised and distributed
- insist that the class awaits the arrival of the last pupil before entering the room
- establish silence outside the classroom before pupils enter
- separate known trouble-makers and locate them in pre-determined places

Some examples of pupils' intended learning outcomes might be:

- play a more active part in group discussion
- use a new piece of equipment effectively
- apply a mathematical rule in new circumstances
- learn a new song
- recall five main facts concerning the industry of the North East
- compare the effects of the Viking and Roman invasions of Britain

- know the names of the main bones in the human skeleton and relate them to their function
- read a passage publicly with clarity and meaning.

In setting objectives for your own aims and the learning outcomes of your pupils make sure that you are being realistic in what you expect of them and yourself.

Remember
Always be fair with yourself. If you have any doubts about your expectations, check them out with a colleague whose greater experience you trust.

Remember
At a minimum, discuss your self-appraisal process with a trusted colleague.

---

3 Agree your criteria for effectiveness before reflecting on your work

In the previous ground rule the objectives were described with considerable detail. Only by working in this way is it possible to get a clear insight into the effectiveness of your work.

Having now listed a set of objectives, you need to decide the criteria by which you will judge the quality of your work. The criteria should be as simple and unambiguous as you can define them. Ideally there should be few of them but they should cover the main objectives with which you are working. The following example will illustrate the point:

Objective: to gain class control more readily at the start of a lesson.

Sub-objectives	*Related criteria*
1 Arrive in class before the first pupil	1A Present in classroom 5 minutes before start of lesson
2 Have materials organised	2A Materials arranged in working order and in sets for each pupil
	2B Materials distributed to each desk
	2C Put names of known trouble-makers on sets of materials at pre-determined desks

3 Insist that class awaits last pupil's arrival before entering classroom	3A Stand at closed classroom door
	3B Record time
	3C Pupils line up in orderly fashion
	3D Order maintained whilst awaiting late arrivals
4 Establish silence outside classroom	4A Record time and inform pupils of time
	4B Pupils enter in silence
5 Separate known trouble-makers and locate at pre-determined desks	5A 'Trouble-makers' remain sitting in identified places

This procedure of identifying detailed objectives and the criteria for determining their achievement is very time-consuming. It cannot be applied to every lesson but it is the only way to get beyond a subconscious level of awareness based solely on impressions of effectiveness. The detailed approach presented will take you beyond impressions to a fuller and more objective view which will justify the extra time and effort required if your goal is to gain greater insight into the quality of your work.

Remember
You do not need to operate at a high level of detailed planning of objectives and criteria for measurement in every lesson

---

4 Whenever possible involve another teacher in the process

There are many reasons why you should involve an experienced and trusted colleague in your self-appraisal system:

- it will increase your level of objectivity
- it will allow an alternative view of each stage in the system
- it will provide an alternative insight into what is acceptable as a professional standard
- it will help to keep your approach at a realistic and achievable level
- it may lead to reciprocal working relationships, allowing greater insight into alternative ways of working.

Self-appraisal is a time-consuming and rewarding activity which lends itself well to sharing experiences. Ideally the process should operate on a reciprocal basis with a trusted, experienced colleague so that at each stage in the process you can check the clarity, purpose and value of your own system against someone else's understanding.

It is not necessary for your colleague to be present during the lessons from which you are collecting information. But it is important that you go through your planning, your objectives, and your criteria before applying them; and then discuss the outcomes, the analysis, your conclusion and your next action. Clearly this requires time and this should be allowed for and built into shared planning.

5 Allow adequate time for preparation, collecting evidence, analysing your information and discussing each of these stages with a trusted, experienced colleague

The overall time required very much depends upon your chosen approach. However, at least in the early stages of developing your approach, allow considerable time for planning, preparation, and discussion.

As a general rule start your planning one week in advance. At this stage identify the class you will use as the basis of your work (see 'Do not use a single sample' on p. 49). Decide the time during which you will be collecting information and note the work you will be covering. A number of the tools discussed in chapter 5 describe in detail the specific time requirements suggested for your personal planning. In general you should allow ten minutes for identifying your objectives/ intended outcomes and stating these within your chosen system for collecting evidence of your performance. You may then need up to ten minutes after the particular teaching session to complete your observations of the outcomes, your initial analysis of your work and identification of those 'questions to self' which will form the key points of your process of reflection. Finally, you will need up to a further twenty minutes to go through this information with your chosen colleague.

If this amount of time seems too much, and out of proportion to the actual time you taught the lesson, remind yourself of the purpose and value of your self-appraisal and the part it is playing in strengthening the quality of your work, and of your capacity to describe this work with accuracy and objectivity.

6 Always be fair with yourself and keep things in perspective

In general we are far more practised at negative criticism of our own ability and performance than we are at recognising and allowing ourselves to believe in our successes. It is, therefore, very important to keep a balanced approach to self-analysis in order to prevent a slide into self-denigration at the expense of recognising what is good about your work. Also be fair to yourself in your choice of teaching group and teaching task.

The earlier section 'Do not use a single sample' drew attention to the limitations of working with only one group. This section reminds you that in choosing your group you need to ensure that you have realistic expectations of success, especially if you are in your early years of teaching, either as a probationary teacher or a teacher who has just changed schools. The approaches to self-appraisal described in this book are intended to be supportive and developmental. They are not written for heroines or heroes who are hell bent on fighting lost battles. So if you have one or more groups who give you severe difficulties, do not focus on them at the start of your self-appraisal. Work up to them so that you are first familiar with the approaches you are using. In particular have courage to trust the experienced colleague you are already working with before tackling any group or curriculum area that is giving you a problem. In this way it will be easier to identify routes to success; you will be far less likely to get drawn into over-reactive, negative self-criticism.

If, in reading this section, you recognise yourself as already in this position of negative self-criticism, talk about it to the trusted, experienced colleague you intend to work with, as her reactions will be helpful to you, both in clarifying your views of your work, and your views of her.

Finally, always keep things in perspective. The self-appraisal process we are describing is important to you; it will help you to clarify your view of the quality of your work and it will strengthen your professional resolve because you will have a clearer insight into the outcomes of your teaching. But do not get drawn into the trap of over-emphasising this aspect of your professional role. It is far more important to be an effective teacher than an effective self-appraiser. The process is time-consuming; do not let it interfere with the quality of your lesson preparation or the process itself may become your cause for concern.

7 Find a way of making your self-knowledge explicit

Too often, as teachers, we operate at the level of tacit understanding. In our interactions with other teachers, either casually in the staffroom or purposefully in our professional planning and delivery, we do not make explicit the meaning of that which we expect to happen or achieve. In general terms we are not good at describing the educational process in simple language and we too readily shroud ourselves in complex language or jargon, often riddled with acronyms, making our language unintelligible to ourselves, let alone the clients we serve. So, in focusing on your own self-analysis, always try to describe what has happened; what you have done; and your feelings about these things, in simple, direct language. If, against your objective to introduce small group discussion work, your outcome was a noisy, unproductive and un-controlled mess, describe it this way, then look for reasons why this happened and describe them in straightforward terms too. In this way you will come to a clearer view of the explanations for the outcome. It is then vital that you talk about these with your trusted colleague and write them in your record of the work, in clear explicit terms. As well as a key part of the self-appraisal process, this is also a rehearsal of your growing knowledge and skills which will become increasingly important especially if you are in, or aspire to, more responsible positions of leadership.

8 Do not put too much pressure on yourself — focus on one or two aspects of your work that need attention

This rule relates closely to the earlier one 'be fair to yourself'. In this specific case it refers to the aspects of your work that lie at the heart of your self-appraisal. In choosing your focus of attention take care not to be over-ambitious in your selection. It is far more helpful to you to cover a single area well than to risk discouraging failure through an over-ambitious range of expectations. Our advice is simple: at the start choose only one approach and one single aspect of your work. In choosing the approach look carefully at the detailed attention it will require and the extent to which it readily matches the area of your need. In the last section of this chapter is a list of different aspects of teaching. You may well find the list helpful in focusing your attention on a single aspect that is for you a current priority. Of course, with increasing confidence in the use of a single tool, you should introduce other tools, and as your experience grows so you will find you are able to use them in combi-nation with each other, thereby broadening your insight into the quality of your work.

9 Use appropriate tools to collect your evidence

In chapter 5 we describe a wide range of approaches. Some of them are very flexibile and open up a large number of opportunities for reflection. For example, the use of a video camera gives you great scope since you can view the same piece of recorded teaching and consider many dif-ferent aspects of your work.

Other tools are more specific. For example, the professional space diagram (see p. 74) can be used in a number of different settings, but its main outcomes will only reflect the quality of adult interactions and relationships.

Then there are the approaches that are more specific to a particular task. For example, time line approaches (see p. 100) have little value outside of establishing overall patterns of performance and time sequences.

10 Be honest with yourself

If you have taken the other 'rules' into account you will have chosen to work with a class of pupils with whom you have reasonable confidence and expectation of success. You will be covering an area of curriculum in which you are adequately prepared, using methods of approach in which you have reasonable confidence. You will also have chosen an aspect of your work to increase your insight into personal performance and your scope for development.

In terms of your preparation you will have spent time writing your objectives, intended outcomes and the criteria you will use to judge the product of your reflective process. You will also have prepared any recording sheets you may require or have set up the video recording camera if you have chosen to use one.

Your trusted colleague will also be aware of your preparations and have an expectation to meet with you to discuss the outcomes of your work.

All of this build-up will have helped you to be objective in what you do and say about your performance, and your degree of honesty in accepting your own evidence will control the ultimate value of the process. Allow yourself to accept both the success and failure in what you find.

11 Whenever possible tie in your self-appraisal to your school's organisational appraisal

The summary to the section 'The contexts in which I work' describes the teacher as an all-round professional serving the needs of learners, fellow teachers, headteacher, governors, parents and the local community. Education will always provide a wide range of career opportunities for development of effective teachers both in terms of prospects and the challenge of the classroom and the mastery of skills to provide even more effective learning opportunities for pupils.

In considering personal aims and objectives we suggest that you keep in mind the structure outlined on the opposite page.

The diagram attempts to represent the interaction between personal aims and objectives, self-appraisal and formal appraisal and the part each element plays in the other two.

Self-appraisal prepares the appraisee to be in a stronger position to enter the appraisal process supported by clearer insights into the quality

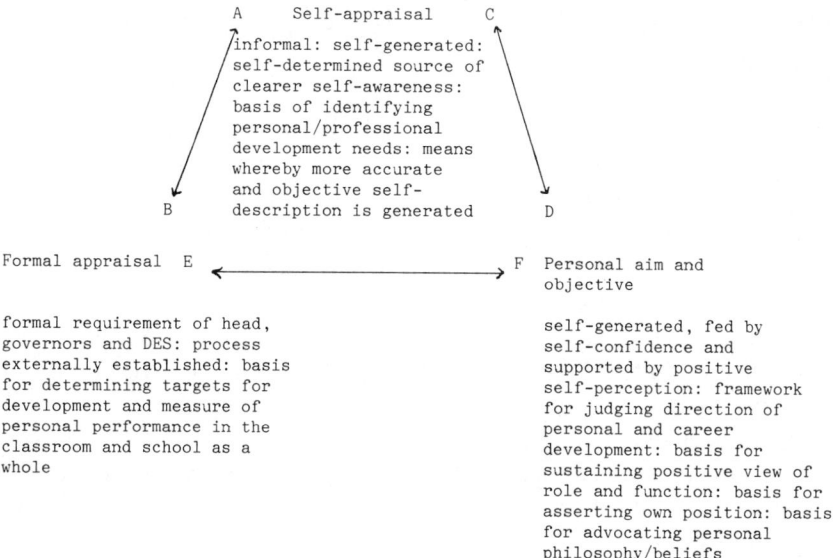

A   Self-appraisal   C

```
informal: self-generated:
self-determined source of
clearer self-awareness:
basis of identifying
personal/professional
development needs: means
whereby more accurate
and objective self-
description is generated
```

B   D

Formal appraisal E ⟵⟶ F Personal aim and objective

```
formal requirement of head,
governors and DES: process
externally established: basis
for determining targets for
development and measure of
personal performance in the
classroom and school as a
whole
```

```
self-generated, fed by
self-confidence and
supported by positive
self-perception: framework
for judging direction of
personal and career
development: basis for
sustaining positive view of
role and function: basis for
asserting own position: basis
for advocating personal
philosophy/beliefs
```

of personal worth and understanding of personal and professional development needs.

The formal appraisal process in turn benefits from this information and in return creates the necessary structure of relating self-perception to the perception of others, thereby reinforcing shared perceptions and challenging differences in perception. Schools' formal appraisal systems also provide the rigour of required attention to needs in stated time frameworks. The process is both the sharp edge of professional judgement on performance and the source of personal and professional support for growth and development.

Personal aims and objectives relate essentially to both processes. They provide a clear statement of personal expectations and aspirations as part of the formal appraisal process. They inform the appraiser in so far as they give insight to the match or mismatch with the teacher's current level of performance, and hence assist the appraiser in helping the appraisee to gain an accurate picture of their potential and future capacity for greater responsibility. Statements of aims and objectives also provide necessary guidelines for self-appraisal and act as a source of drive and motivation for the appraisee.

In return self-appraisal supports the growth of self-confidence to reassess personal aims and objectives if they are too limited; or to accept them when they are truly challenging. The formal appraisal process, in the hands of a skilled and sensitive appraiser, further assists the appropriate adjustment of personal aims and objectives by helping us to see more clearly how others see us and value us.

What factors prevent teachers from achieving their full potential?

Throughout this chapter there is the hitherto unstated principle that self-appraisal requires teachers to accept responsibility for their own personal and professional development. As with pupils in the classroom-learning situation, teachers cannot develop unless they have the drive, purpose, stimulation and motivation to do so. To some degree control over success or failure here lies outside the individual and rests within the system in which the individual operates. However, the teacher as an experienced adult, unlike the pupil, cannot abrogate her responsibility. She must assess the part she can play in changing the situation and circumstances in which she finds herself. Therefore, in working through this section you should focus your attention on your own responsibilities as well as those of others whom you may too readily be willing to blame for your situation.

A vital factor you need to appreciate about self-appraisal and formal appraisal systems is the need for internal motivation. It is generally accepted that motivation cannot be imposed on an individual and that most individuals' goals are needs-seeking. It is, therefore, necessary for you to be clear about your needs so that you can play a full part in agreeing what they are within the school's formal system of appraisal and ensuring that they are attainable. Maslow's[5] theory of personality and motivation can help us here. It is both relevant in general terms and appropriate to teaching. In the diagram opposite we have set out Maslow's view of the levels of need and related these to self (personal) and to the role of teacher (organisational/task).

It is our view that physiological and safety needs are just as essential within the role of teacher as they are when seen in personal terms. As a teacher you need to feel secure. You need to be safe in your knowledge and skills, and not under threat. Similarly just as a person needs to feel that she belongs in the sense of family or group, so too within the school's organisation there is a group, including pupils, colleagues, senior staff, governors and advisers, which represent the 'professional family'.

With this situation in mind there is a key point of agreement between Maslow's theory and education and this is the premise that when needs at a basic level are met they no longer act as a source of motivation. If we accept this then there are potential problems for you as you approach a realisation of your own effectiveness. It is possible to observe many teachers who consolidate at the safety level and make no attempt to move on to a team situation, nor to gain a wider base of professional respect. It is essential, therefore, that you do not perceive the process of self-appraisal merely as a means of confirming your current level of

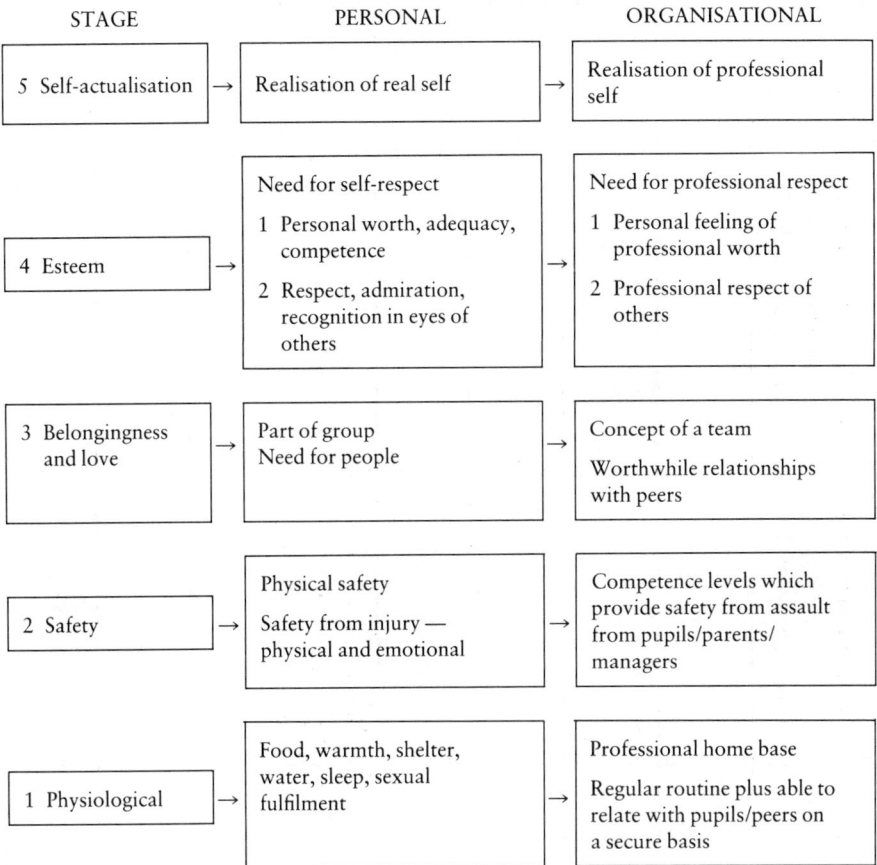

STAGE	PERSONAL	ORGANISATIONAL
5 Self-actualisation	Realisation of real self	Realisation of professional self
4 Esteem	Need for self-respect 1 Personal worth, adequacy, competence 2 Respect, admiration, recognition in eyes of others	Need for professional respect 1 Personal feeling of professional worth 2 Professional respect of others
3 Belongingness and love	Part of group Need for people	Concept of a team Worthwhile relationships with peers
2 Safety	Physical safety Safety from injury — physical and emotional	Competence levels which provide safety from assault from pupils/parents/managers
1 Physiological	Food, warmth, shelter, water, sleep, sexual fulfilment	Professional home base Regular routine plus able to relate with pupils/peers on a secure basis

effectiveness, but rather as a process of constantly identifying further needs for development so that you can progress as a professional and fulfil your potential.

The list below sets out factors that can get in the way of teachers reaching their full potential. In reading the list consider each item in terms of the following questions:

1 Does this apply directly to me?
2 Does this apply to those for whom I have responsibility?
3 Do I have a personal responsibility to do something about this?

As you go down the list mark in the responses appropriate to yourself. When you have completed the list add other factors which you consider have been omitted. Finally, go through the list and identify your top three priority items for action. Mark these in the right-hand column of the table. At the first opportunity discuss these priorities with your trusted, experienced colleague and see if you can see ways forward for action.

	Does this apply directly to me?	Does this apply to those for whom I have responsibility?	Do I have a personal responsibility to do something about this?	Priority
Have run out of steam, goals achieved, no new goals				
Personal problems or change in life situation				
Feel personally criticised				
Loss of self-confidence				
Stress				
Poor personal relationships				
Lack of energy, drive, good health				
Generation gap				

	Does this apply directly to me?	Does this apply to those for whom I have responsibility?	Do I have a personal responsibility to do something about this?	Priority
Fear of exposure of personal inadequacies				
Other interests				
Lack of job satisfaction				
Lack of genuine interest in subject(s) taught				
Lack of knowledge of subject				
Uncertainty about objective of subject				
Unprepared for change of role				
Lack of leadership				

Loss of belief in task								
Poor class control								
Too many roles/responsibilies								
Isolation/staff fragmentation								
Being blocked by established senior staff								
Criticism from superiors								
No concensus over school rules and procedures								
No concensus over educational goals and values								
Poor communication								

	Does this apply directly to me?	Does this apply to those for whom I have responsibility?	Do I have a personal responsibility to do something about this?	Priority
Lack of machinery for participation				
Disruptive behaviour in the classroom				
Promotion blocked				
Unsuitability for teaching				
Poor working conditions and limited resources				
System not relevant to needs of students				
Lack of parental support				
Threat of closure, redundancy, reorganisation, redeployment				

Poor appointments							
Lack of provision for least academic students							
Uncertain about purpose of education							
Isolation of school from wider community							
Public criticism, scapegoating							
Extreme behavioural problems							
Teachers' cultural values differ from those of young people							
Lack of parental understanding, interest and support							

5 Different ways of appraising myself

Introduction

This chapter is concerned solely with practical ways of gaining greater self-awareness for teachers. Most of the activities centre on classroom work though some deal with the wider issues of adult relationships in school, career progression and personal marketing. Each of the activities is designed to stand alone but many fit together in a developing sequence, and this is made clear by cross-references within the text.

The majority of the procedures require recorded responses and throughout the chapter charts and recording sheets are provided for this purpose. All of these are copyright-free to the owner of the book who is advised to photocopy them rather than use the originals in the book.

Some of the activities require classroom observation. These are more effective when undertaken with a trusted colleague. Better still, if it is possible to video record the lessons you can observe them at your leisure and still have the advantage of working with a colleague.

In the following activities (V) alongside the heading denotes the advantage of video recording.

Professional space diagram

Though the quality of teaching and learning is the main determinant by which most teachers are judged in their contribution to school life, there are other ways in which major contributions are made. Many of these contributions come through the various adult relationships that exist in schools.

This activity will assist you to identify more precisely your range of personal and professional relationships in school.

Procedure

1   List the names of the adults in your school with whom you have a working professional relationship. The list may include members of

the non-teaching staff, governors, members of the education department or parents of your pupils. Whoever the members of your list may be, the one thing they have in common is their relationship with you.

2　　　Using the professional space diagram Sheet provided, write the initials of the people you have already listed, placing them at distances away from the dot at the centre of the sheet that represents you so that the distance represents the closeness of your relationship and the extent to which you know and rely upon the person in your working situation. As you add initials to your sheet you may well find yourself having to reassess the position you chose for a person previously placed on the sheet. Not all the people on your original list will have been there because of the positive nature of your relationship with them. Or if you only listed those who are your 'friends', then go back to your list and add those whom you failed to see as part of this activity because you assumed this was purely in terms of friendship.

3　　　If you have extended your list, add these initials to your sheet. You may now have a paper with initials spread across the sheet — some towards the edge reflecting the superficial level of their connection or limited knowledge and reliance, others very close to you because you work closely with them, know them well and rely on them considerably.

4　　　Consider the overall pattern. Are there any groups of initials where the people have things in common with each other as well as with you? If there are, put a line around them to cluster them. (You may need to reposition some of them.)

5　　　Consider the pattern of names in terms of roles. Which of those people on your list are responsible for your line management? Mark these up in a bracket with large letters (TM) for teacher manager.

If you are the line manager for some of the people on your sheet look carefully where they are positioned. Are they grouped in any way? If they are, put a line around them, or reposition them if you feel they should have been grouped. Mark up each of the people for whom you are line manager with large letters (LM) in a bracket.

Do you consider any of the people on your sheet to be your friends? Are they too arranged in a group? Should they have been closer in a group? Rearrange them if you feel they should. Mark these people up in a bracket with a large (F).

6　　　Consider the whole group in terms of support. Here we must be clear in our distinction between support and friendship. Those whom we consider our friends may well reciprocate the warmth of companionship, shared activities, pleasures and insights into personal, even confidential, aspects of our life beyond school as well as school life. Others who do not relate to us in this way may, however, represent key people in whom we have trust, and on whom we rely heavily for assistance and guidance in our professional roles. Such colleagues provide

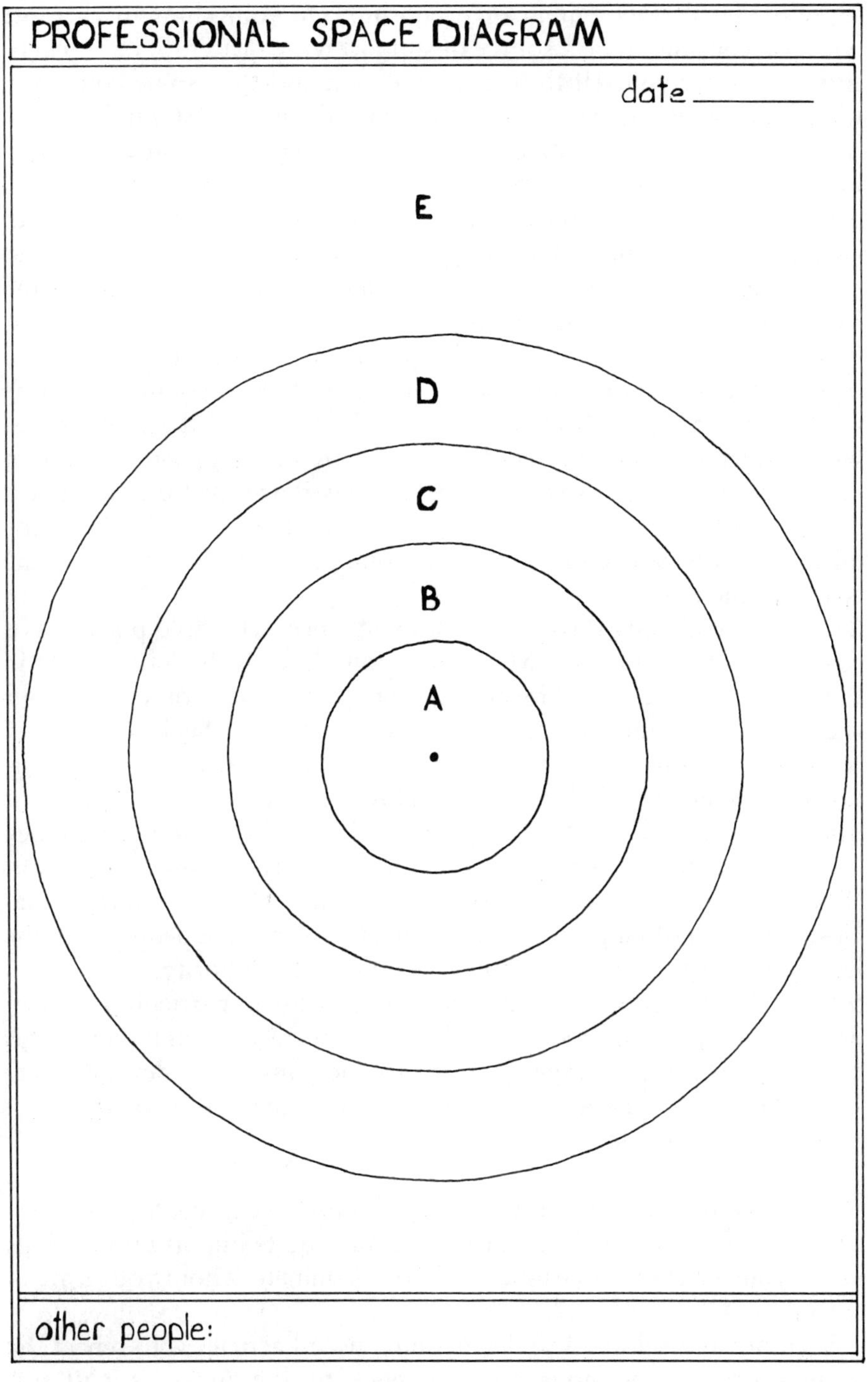

PROFESSIONAL SPACE DIAGRAM

date _____

E

D

C

B

A

•

other people:

support outside the context of friendship. On your chart mark those who you consider to be a source of support with a letter (S) in brackets. If you consider yourself to be a source of support for some colleagues mark the position of these colleagues with the letters (SG) in brackets. Your professional space diagram will almost certainly represent a complex pattern of inter-relationships. Such patterns are seldom stable. They are subject to internal mobility brought about by the tide of changing relationships which all groups demonstrate over time, due to colleagues taking up new posts, both inside and outside the school, and by the introduction of new staff.

7   Consider again the people placed on your chart. Are any of them in the process of movement? Are any of them coming closer as sources of support or friendship? Mark the initials of these colleagues with an arrow pointing inwards to the centre of the paper. Are any of the people less close to you than in the past? Are they providing less support? Is their professional relationship diminishing? Mark the initials of these people with an arrow pointing outwards away from the centre of the page.

8   Now identify those people on your sheet who hold positions of seniority within the staff. Mark these initials with the letters (FA) in brackets to denote their formal authority. Are there others on your sheet who have informal authority within the staff? Such people may not hold positions of management responsibility, they may not be post-holders or heads of department. However, when in a formal or informal group setting their presence is noted by the majority and they are a factor which affects the behaviour and responses of the staff. When they speak they are normally accorded both the courtesy and close attention of all present. Mark the initials of these people with the letters (IA) in brackets to denote their informal authority.

9   Finally, and in the light of the last factor in particular, is there anyone not on the sheet but who has authority over you and therefore is in a position to exert influence over you and your future development? Note the initials of these people in a box at the corner of the sheet headed 'other people'.

The exercise you have been through should have given you considerable food for thought. You have made some quite important decisions about your teaching colleagues and other adults to whom you relate in school.

Such pictures seldom stay fixed, and a useful activity is to repeat the same procedure, without any reference to the previous patterns, allowing you then to compare the patterns to see what changes, if any, have occurred.

10   Using the completed chart ask yourself the following questions:

1 What is the range of your professional relationships in school?
2 Are you satisfied with this range of relationships?
3 What is the range and level of support you receive in school?
4 Are you satisfied with this range and level of support?
5 Do you have a range of friendships in school?
6 Are you satisfied by this range of in-school friendship?
7 How closely do you relate to authority figures in school?
8 Do you wish to change this in any way?
9 Do you have informal authority of your own in school?
10 How do you use this informal authority?
11 Do you have formal authority in school?
12 How do you use this formal authority?
13 What changes, if any, would you like to see on your professional space diagram? Record these on your sheet and keep it safe for the time when you repeat the activity.

The example of a professional space diagram overleaf comes from a young teacher in his third year of secondary teaching. The comments have been added to provide an indication of the reasons for the pattern of relationships. The diagram raises a number of questions, some of which you may find interesting to apply to your own situation.

There is only one set of initials in the inner circle (A). Does this mean the teacher is unable to form or maintain very close professional relationships? Is this limited close support a problem? A number of formal authority (FA) figures are positioned in the outer circles. Does this indicate a rejection of formal authority? Does it indicate a need for some urgent action to rectify what may become a problem in later career?

In general the teacher appears to be well supported. The headteacher and a senior head of department are sources of close support; two colleagues offer friendship and support and two other colleagues who joined the school at the same time offer support. Is it possible to maintain effective professional relationships with so many different people offering support?

The school secretary and caretaker are occupying interesting positions. Are these people important in our professional relationships?

Pupil space diagram (class space diagram)

This activity is designed to help you identify and describe the pupil/pupil and pupil/teacher interactions that operate when you are teaching a specific class of pupils, and the variations in these relationships from class to class. You may find this procedure helpful in pinpointing the

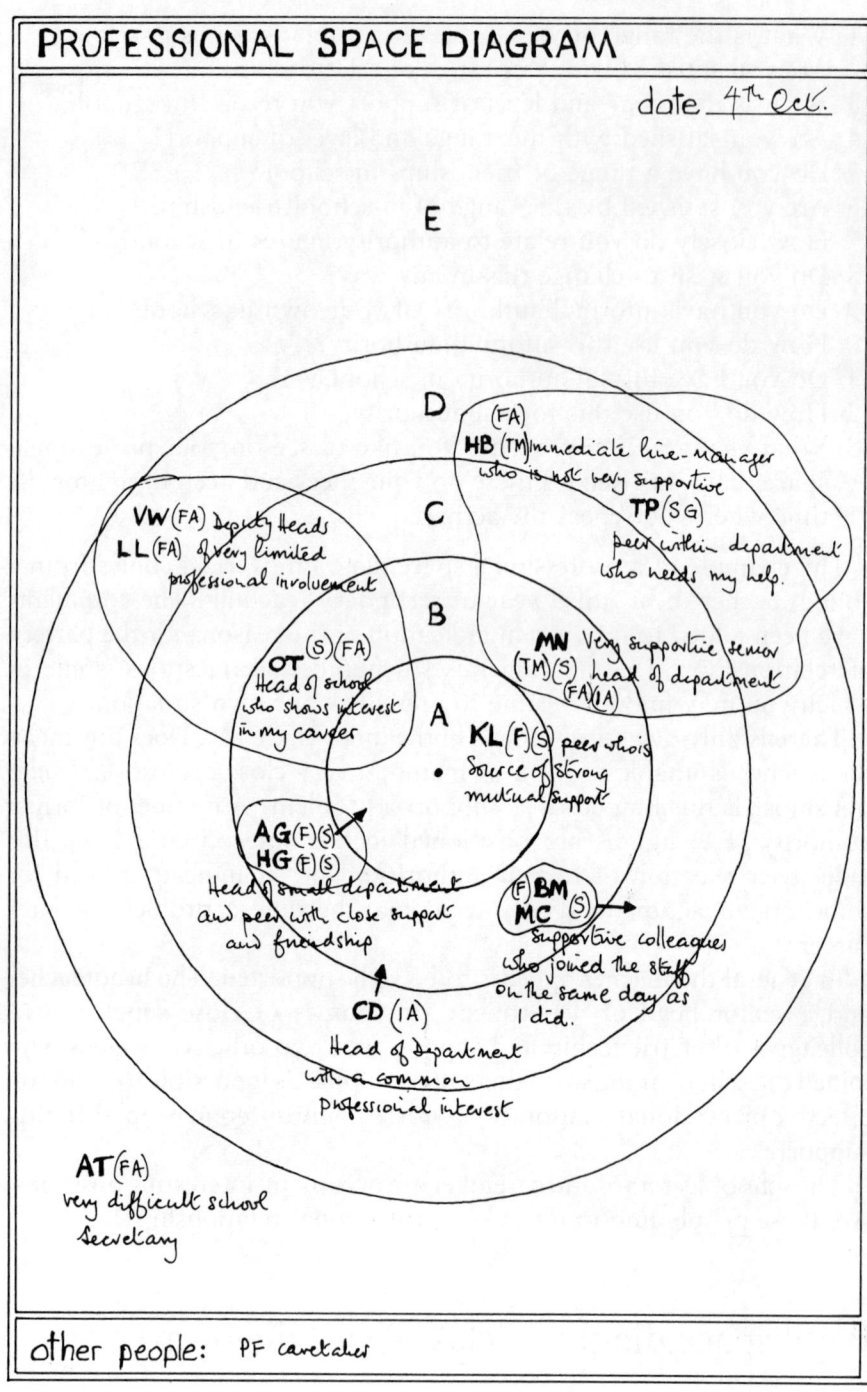

PROFESSIONAL SPACE DIAGRAM

date _4th Oct._

E

D

C

B

A

(FA)
HB (TM) immediate line-manager
who is not very supportive

TP (SG)
peer within department
who needs my help.

VW (FA) Deputy Heads
LL (FA) of very limited
professional involvement

MN Very supportive senior
(TM) (S) head of department
(FA) (IA)

OT (S) (FA)
Head of school
who shows interest
in my career

KL (F) (S) peer who is
source of strong
mutual support

AG (F) (S)
HG (F) (S)
Head of small department
and peer with close support
and friendship

(F) **BM** (S)
MC
supportive colleagues
who joined the staff
on the same day as
I did.

CD (IA)
Head of department
with a common
professional interest

AT (FA)
very difficult school
secretary

other people: PF caretaker

PUPIL SPACE DIAGRAM

Name of class/teaching group _____ date _____

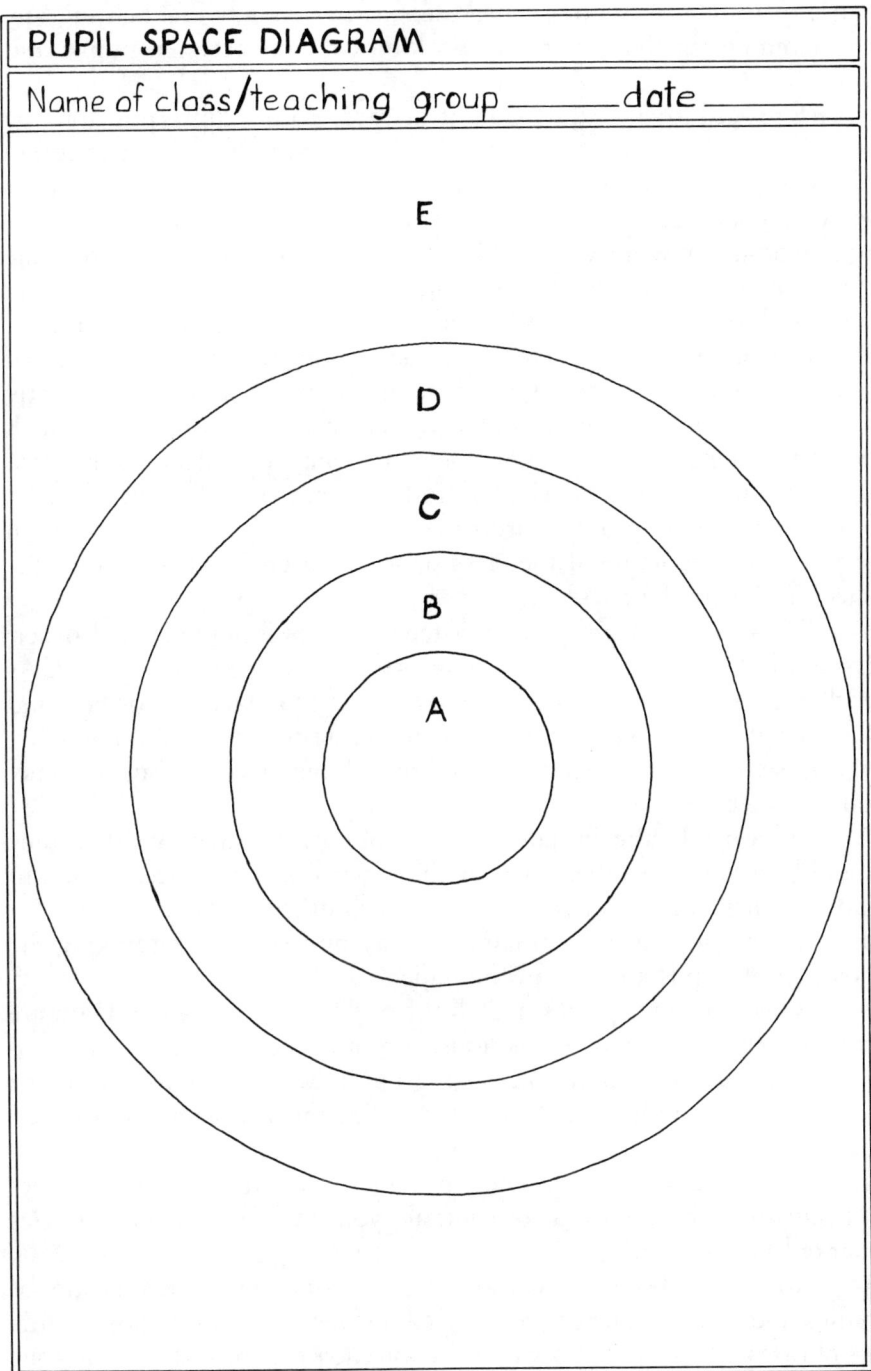

cause of problem situations, if these exist, as well as highlighting any shortcomings in the pattern of working contacts between pupils and yourself.

The procedure is quite straightforward. You simply position the initials of all the pupils in your class on a copy of the Pupil Space Diagram Sheet provided, so that their distance from the centre represents your view of your effective working relationship with each pupil, ie, those with whom you work well will be at the centre of the paper within the inner circle. Those with whom you have the least effective working relationship will be around the edge of the paper in the outer ring. Ideally you should complete a class space diagram sheet for each of your teaching groups to gain a general picture of how you currently view your working relationships. Better still you should work with another teacher in whom you have trust and confidence, who also teaches some of the same classes, and compare your diagrams.

Use the following procedure to complete your pupil space diagram sheet. Write the name of the class or teaching group at the top of the sheet in the space provided.

1   Work strictly from your register of names in alphabetical order. Do not be tempted to place the names as they come to your mind. As each pupil is placed, first decide in which ring to place him or her, and then decide where within the ring you will write the initials. You may, of course, decide to place the initial on a boundary line, but this may cause difficulties for you later.

2   As you add the initials of other pupils, consider whether they should be close to others within the same ring or adjacent rings to indicate their regular interaction with each other in class.

3   As you add further initials you may find yourself rethinking the position of pupils already on the paper.

4   When you have positioned all the pupils in your class and you are content with their relative positions, complete the next part of the procedure. Focus your attention on the pupils whose initials are in the inner circle A and list words which describe the characteristics of their behaviour, attitude and personal organisation in the column marked A on the group characteristics sheet provided. Repeat this process of description for the pupils whose initials you have put in those circles marked B, C, D and E.

5   Now consider your working relationship with each group of pupils and use the teacher/group relationships sheet to list those words or phrases which best describe this, for each group, in terms of your level of:

- control over their work and behaviour
- motivation of their performance in work

```
┌─────────────────────────────────────────────────────────────┐
│ ┌─────────────────────────────────────────────────────────┐ │
│ │ GROUP CHARACTERISTICS SHEET                             │ │
│ ├─────────────────────────────────────────────────────────┤ │
│ │ Name of class/teaching group_____ date _____     │ │
│ ├───────┬─────────────────────────────────────────────────┤ │
│ │ group │ characteristics of group—behaviour/attitude/organisation │
│ ├───────┼─────────────────────────────────────────────────┤ │
│ │   A   │                                                 │ │
│ ├───────┼─────────────────────────────────────────────────┤ │
│ │   B   │                                                 │ │
│ ├───────┼─────────────────────────────────────────────────┤ │
│ │   C   │                                                 │ │
│ ├───────┼─────────────────────────────────────────────────┤ │
│ │   D   │                                                 │ │
│ ├───────┼─────────────────────────────────────────────────┤ │
│ │   E   │                                                 │ │
│ └───────┴─────────────────────────────────────────────────┘ │
└─────────────────────────────────────────────────────────────┘
```

- maintenance of their on-task performance
- matching your expectations to their capabilities
- organisation and relevance of the work you have prepared.

By this stage you have accumulated considerable information about your pupils, their characteristics in groups and your working relationship with them. If you feel that this analysis has clarified your working relationships with these pupils then we suggest you go one stage further.

This next procedure is designed to map the pattern of pupil distribution in your classroom to see if there are other features of your classroom organisation and management that may be affecting your work as you have recorded it on the teacher/group relationship sheet. 6   For this procedure use the classroom layout sheet provided on page 81. First, draw the outline of your classroom, as seen from above, in which you normally teach the group you have been analysing. Show the position of the door or doors and any windows, cupboards or shelves around the perimeter of the room. Now draw in the position of your desk and chair and the pupils' desks and chairs or benches. 7   Refer now to your group space diagram sheet and position a letter A for each pupil in group A to show where they normally sit in your class. Repeat this for all the other pupils who are arranged in groups B, C, D and E on your group space diagram sheet. Now write the letter T

TEACHER/GROUP RELATIONSHIPS SHEET

Name of class/teaching group _____   date _____

group	control over work and behaviour	motivation of performance in work	maintenance of on-task performance	matching expectations to capabilities	organisation and relevance of work
A					
B					
C					
D					
E					

CLASSROOM LAYOUT SHEET

Name of class teaching group _____ date _____

in the classroom spaces that you normally or most frequently occupy. If you are sure that you are completely mobile when teaching this group you will have placed Ts in all the spaces. If you tend to occupy only part of the classroom, then this should be reflected in local clusters of Ts.

Using this sheet as the basis of your answers:

- what do you notice about the distribution of pupils in your classroom?
- what is the relationship between the distribution of pupils in different categories A to E and the classroom spaces you tend to occupy?
- how does the pattern of pupil distribution positively or negatively contribute to the effectiveness of your work with this class?
- how does your pattern of classroom space occupation positively or negatively contribute to the effectiveness of your work?

As a result of this work you may have identified some actions which would help to add to the quality of your work with the class or classes you have analysed. Use the group space action sheet provided to write out these actions in the form of decisions and the objectives you associate with them. For example, you may decide to move a pupil you have identified as reasonably motivated but at risk from negative influences into a particular group of well-motivated pupils with the objective of improving that pupil's performance. On the other hand perhaps your action will be to separate pupils known to be poorly motivated or a source of distraction and disruption with the objective of reducing their impact on the rest of the class and improving their individual patterns of work.

If your intended actions concern your own classroom movements then consider using the next procedure 'classroom mobility mapping' before taking your actions, since this will undoubtedly give you more detailed information about your own movements.

Classroom activity/mobility mapping (V)

This procedure can be operated in one of two ways either with a partner or using video equipment. If you are working with a partner then he or she can record your pattern of movements directly onto a recording sheet during the lesson. This has the added bonus of their overall awareness of the activities and interactions. However, it also has the drawback that their presence will probably have an effect both on you and the class.

The alternative is to use a video camera and recorder and this is the recommended approach. It has the merit of complete objectivity since the camera sees and records everything, whilst at the same time allowing

GROUP SPACE ACTION SHEET

Name of class/teaching group _____ date _____

objective(s) of specific action(s)	action(s) to be taken

replay for detailed analysis which, of course, can involve your working partner. The limitations are the availability of equipment and a lack of appropriate classroom location in which to place the equipment. If your school does not have its own video camera and recorder, see if the headteacher will arrange for you to borrow equipment, either from another school or from the LEA through its resources centre or teachers' centre.

The best equipment for this purpose is an integrated camera recorder. They are very compact, require little space or support, and have a less distracting influence on pupils.

For the sake of completeness both approaches to the procedure are described below.

Working with a partner

Using the classroom activity/mobility mapping sheet provide your partner with an aerial view of your classroom showing clearly all the pieces of furniture, the blackboard, doors, windows and cupboards etc. Try and make it as accurate as possible. Ideally your partner should also have a stopwatch, but most digital wrist watches provide this facility and you may not need a specialist stopwatch.

The procedure is very simple but also very demanding of your partner. At each minute of the lesson your partner will record on your classroom map the point which denotes your position in the classroom at that time. These positions are marked by the time recorded. Also in the section of the sheet marked 'record of activities' your partner records your precise activity at that time. A single word or short phrase is sufficient at the time of recording. Working in this way your partner builds up an accurate record of your classroom movements in relation to the activities you are performing throughout the lesson. Before the lesson begins make sure that your partner knows exactly what to do and agree the precise moment when the record will commence. Ideally this should coincide with the start of the lesson.

Below is a completed classroom activity/mobility mapping sheet showing the kind of movements and comments which may appear.

Working with a video camera and recorder

Remember
An integrated camera/recorder is the most suitable equipment for this purpose.

CLASSROOM ACTIVITY/MOBILITY MAPPING SHEET

Name of class/teaching group _____   date _____

record of activities

TIME	ACTIVITY	TIME	ACTIVITY
0		30	
1		31	
2		32	
3		33	
4		34	
5		35	
6		36	
7		37	
8		38	
9		39	
10		40	
11		41	
12		42	
13		43	
14		44	
15		45	
16		46	
17		47	
18		48	
19		49	
20		50	
21		51	
22		52	
23		53	
24		54	
25		55	
26		56	
27		57	
28		58	
29		59	

record of mobility

classroom perimeter →

86

CLASSROOM ACTIVITY/MOBILITY MAPPING SHEET

Name of class/teaching group ___ 3MN ___   date 4ᵗʰ Oct

record of activities

TIME	ACTIVITY	TIME	ACTIVITY
0	working to class	30	checking books
1	working, checking books	31	checking books
2	working, checking books	31	introducing development of task
3	working, class starts to arrive	33	developing task
4	controlling class at door	34	developing task
5	controlling class, waiting for silence	35	assisting group with new task
6	settling class	36	assisting group with new task
7	talking to class about behaviours	37	responding to pupils' suggestions
8	reminding class about work for today	38	responding to pupils' suggestions.
9	giving out books	39	whole class active, working well
10	giving out books	40	whole class active, working well
11	dealing with pupils A and B	41	whole class active working well
12	dealing with pupils A and B	42	pupil unwell Ⓒ
13	dealing with pupils A and B	43	pupil unwell class concerned
14	settling whole class	44	pupil unwell, A and B fighting
15	settling whole class	45	sorting out A and B; D taking C to medical room
16	introducing lesson	46	repositioned A in C's place
17	introducing lesson	47	talking at whole class re. behaviour
18	questioning class	48	regaining control and pattern of work
19	question/answer with class	49	full order restored. class working
20	question/answer, reinforcing control A&B	50	keeping close eye on B class working
21	giving more information to class	51	keeping close eye on B class working
22	giving more information to class	52	reinforcing future control over A
23	setting task for class	53	reinforcing future control over A
24	class active on task, checking	54	observing whole class, checking
25	checking, helping individuals	55	checking notes for next lesson.
26	checking, helping individuals	56	checking notes for next lesson.
27	reinforcing control over A and B	57	informing class about next lesson.
28	reinforcing control over A and B	58	informing class about next lesson.
29	checking books.	59	informing class about next lesson.

record of mobility

classroom perimeter ↘

First make sure that you are fully familiar with the use of the equipment before the lesson. Ideally you should make a test to ensure that the picture covers the whole of the classroom and that the sound recording is clear. To get the best coverage, place the camera as high as possible in a corner of the room. If you have a high cupboard or shelves these are ideal locations. If you have to use a camera tripod this will probably distract the class and you will almost certainly need to familiarise your class with the presence of the equipment before using it to analyse your work. If it is possible to set the equipment up without its presence distracting the class this should be done.

Finally if your camera/recorder also has a time-recording facility, use this. It will not only record the image and sound of your lesson but also record the lapse of time in the corner of the picture.

The procedure for recording is simple. Having set up the equipment check that the tape is fully rewound then press the Play/Record button 5 minutes before the pupils are due to arrive then leave it alone, without drawing attention to it during the lesson. After the lesson, and when the pupils have left the room, retrieve the equipment and rewind the tape ready for replay. Replaying the tape should only be done when you have sufficient time to go through the whole lesson undisturbed. The classroom activity/mobility record sheet is completed in exactly the same way as described previously. Try not to stop and start the tape though this may be a great temptation. Instead work your way through steadily, noting the time to register your position in the classroom every minute and keeping a note of your precise activities.

Using the records of the lessons

The mobility map can yield the following information:

a) Pupil contact patterns: The overall pattern of contact with pupils;
b) Teacher space/pupil space: The relative occupation of teacher space and pupil space
c) Teacher tracking: The sequence of movements within the classroom.

a) Pupil contact patterns (V)

Use the classroom mobility analysis grids below to analyse your pupil contact pattern. Place the grid over the outline of your classroom on which you have recorded the pattern of your movements. Zone 1 should overlap the front of your classroom. Put a mark on the analysis grid X to indicate your position for each time record. Add up the totals for each of the zones 1–6, then mark up the front (F) and back (B) of the room on your grid. From this pattern of marks it will be evident how much contact you have had with the various groups of pupils

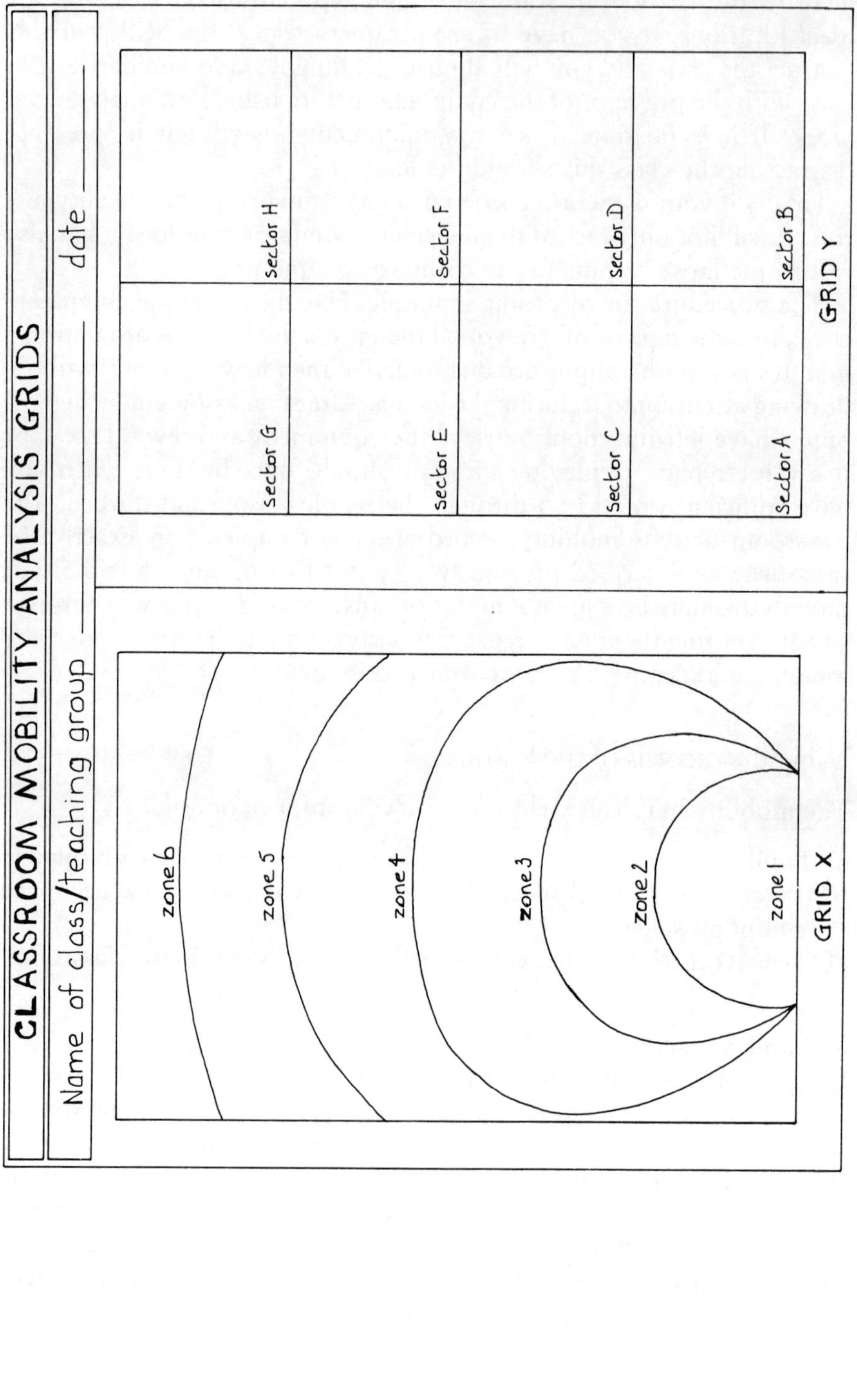

CLASSROOM MOBILITY ANALYSIS GRIDS

Name of class/teaching group _____   date _____

GRID X

zone 6
zone 5
zone 4
zone 3
zone 2
zone 1

GRID Y

Sector G   Sector H
Sector E   Sector F
Sector C   Sector D
Sector A   Sector B

seated around the classroom. You can express this pattern as the time spent in each zone of the room or a percentage of the total lesson time spent in each zone.

- What is the pattern of pupil contact shown by this analysis?
- Which group of pupils receives most of your contact?
- What are the reasons for this?
- Which group of pupils receives least of your contact?
- What are the reasons for this?
- What do you intend to do about your pattern of movement and what are your reasons for wishing to change it?
- When will you repeat the exercise to check the effects of your plan?

b) Teacher space/pupil space (V)

Most learners respond well to personal contact and support especially when delivered in their classroom space. This procedure uses the concept of territorial space. If you have a teacher's desk and chair at the front of the class, and if you regularly draw pupils to you around this desk, it establishes this area as your space, your territory. Similarly it establishes the rest of the room as pupils' territory.

For this procedure use the classroom mobility grid Y. Place the grid over the outline of your classroom on which you have recorded the pattern of your movements. Sectors A and B should correspond to the front of your classroom. Put a mark on grid Y to indicate your position for each time record. Count up the number of marks in each sector and express these totals as percentages of the overall total.

- How territorial are you? Do you spend most of your time around your own desk?
- Why are your movements so restricted?
- How do you gain detailed awareness of the quality of working of those pupils furthest from your territory?
- Who receives most of your personal contact?

c) Teacher tracking (V)

The previous procedures show where you were located at specific moments during a lesson. This is only a set of snapshots and disregards the other contacts made during the time between records and the pattern of movements across the room. This next procedure gives a better indication of your overall pattern of movements. Using your mobility map, draw a line from time record to time record on the recording sheet to connect the sequence of points and use an arrow head to indicate your direction of movement.

- Is there a regular or random pattern to your movements?
- Are you merely responding to pupils' requests for attention, or do you have a predetermined purpose in your classroom movements?
- Are you avoiding particular parts of the classroom, if so, why?

The following procedures are designed to increase your awareness of the patterns of talk in your classroom. The sequence starts with a simple record of the balance between teacher talk, pupil talk and silence, then moves on to a more sophisticated analysis of the types of talk in your classroom. Finally, pupil pursuit is introduced as a method of gauging the experience from the point of view of an individual learner.

d) Teacher talk/pupil talk (V)

For this procedure you will need a copy of the teacher talk/pupil talk recording sheet and, if your video camera/recorder does not have a time display feature, you will also need a stopwatch. Watch the start of the video and decide exactly from which moment you are going to start the timing. Rewind the video to this point and zero the stopwatch. Start the video and stopwatch together.

The recording sheet has two columns under the three headings: Teacher talk, Pupil talk, Silence. In the left-hand column of each pair record the time at which either teacher talk, pupil talk or a silence started. In this way the sequence of times will always go between columns as shown in the example below.

When you have completed the whole recording, fill in the right-hand column under each heading to record the amount of time. To get these figures, simply subtract the figures in sequence:

Teacher talk times are calculated by subtracting time A from time B or time A from time C if teacher talk follows a silence.

Pupil talk times are calculated by subtracting time B from time A where the A time is from the next line down below the B time, and by subtracting time B from time C if pupil talk follows a silence.

Silence times are calculated by subtracting time C from time A or time C from time B dependant on whether or not the silence follows teacher talk or pupil talk.

When you have worked out all of these times, add them up to get the totals for teacher talk, pupil talk, and silence.

- How do the three totals compare?
- How does the teacher talk compare with the pupil talk?
- Do you spend more time talking, or do pupils talk most?
- How much time is spent in silence and how productive is this silence?
- How much opportunity is there for constructive pupil-to-pupil talk?

TEACHER TALK/PUPIL TALK RECORD SHEET

Name of class/teaching group _____ date _____

TEACHER TALK		PUPIL TALK		SILENCE	
starting time	amount of time	starting time	amount of time	starting time	amount of time

TEACHER TALK/PUPIL TALK RECORD SHEET

Name of class/teaching group ___ 3MN ___   date ___ 4th Oct ___

A. TEACHER TALK		B. PUPIL TALK		C. SILENCE	
starting time	amount of time	starting time	amount of time	starting time	amount of time
5.00	14 mins	19.00	2 mins.		
21.00	3 mins			24.00	8 mins
32.00	3 mins			35.00	2 mins
		37.00	2 mins	39.00	5 mins
44.00	6 mins			50.00	
57.00	3 mins.				
TOTAL 29 mins		TOTAL 4 mins		TOTAL 15 mins	

e) Types of classroom talk (V)

Teaching and learning can take many forms. The transmission of information usually requires teacher talk, often in the form of exposition. Similarly, teacher talk is necessary for purposes of classroom organisation and management, giving out instructions, positive intervention, intervention in pupil arguments or distractions, regaining whole class attention and control, giving times checks against tasks, keeping pupils to task, and moving pupils on in their work. Questioning is a vital aspect of teacher talk: the use of open questions to promote involvement and flexibility of response, the use of closed questions to reinforce basic information often through repetition. Teacher questioning can be an abuse of time when closed questioning leads to time-wasting whilst pupils play 'hunt the answer in teacher's head', only to have their quite acceptable answers rejected because they are not exactly the same as the words chosen by the teacher.

Pupil talk is similarly of varied value, and creating and managing opportunities for effective pupil talk is an important part of the work of all teachers. In the crossfire of classroom question and answer between teacher and taught, involvement is too often restricted to the minority, leaving many uninvolved and passive recipients of the process. In open group discussion pupil talk also varies in its on-task level and quality, and it is difficult for the teacher to judge the overall effectiveness of this form of pupil talk without being very mobile in the classroom. An effective approach is to use structured conversations in twos or threes where the talk is governed by a specific sequence of tasks and prompts, always within set time limits. In these circumstances the teacher can more readily ensure effective pupil/pupil on-task talk. The above range of examples of teacher and pupil talk is not exhaustive but it does cover the most frequent forms of classroom interactions.

In this procedure you will record your analysis of the types of talk used in your recorded lesson. You will need a copy of the types of classroom talk recording sheet (see page 94) which lists a range of types of teacher talk and pupil talk. Add other forms of teacher or pupil talk to the list if this is necessary. Use this record sheet in conjunction with the video recording of a lesson. Each time an example of talk is observed in the recording tick one of the boxes against this particular type of talk. Time recording is not necessary in this procedure, though if you are interested in the actual amount of time spent using the different types of talk, you can always note the start times for each as you view the recording. This does, however, become very difficult to sustain and gives little added information. The method is as described above for teacher talk/pupil talk.

TYPES OF CLASSROOM TALK RECORD SHEET

Name of class/teaching group _____   date _____

TEACHER TALK		TOTAL
Introducing work		
Giving instruction		
Exerting control		
Questioning		
Gaining attention		
Giving information		
Intervening between pupils		

PUPIL TALK		
Questioning teacher		
Pupil/pupil on-task talk		
Pupil/pupil off-task talk		
Answering teacher		
Pupil informing class		

Using your recorded evidence:

- Which are the most frequent types of teacher talk in your lesson?
- Did you expect this kind of pattern, and if not, what did you expect?
- Which are the most frequent types of pupil talk?
- Is this pattern what you expected; if not, what did you expect?
- Do you see a need for change; if so, what changes do you intend to make?
- When and how will you check out that you have made your intended changes?

The example on page 96 shows one pattern of teacher talk and pupil talk based on the record illustrated in the classroom activity/mobility mapping sheet shown earlier.

f) Pupil pursuit/on-task levels (V)

This procedure is well known as a means of monitoring the overall effectiveness of classroom learning experiences. The method simply involves close observation of a single pupil throughout a series of lessons. From this information it is possible to evaluate the quality of learning opportunities and experiences on offer.

For the pupose of teacher self-appraisal the procedure is changed slightly, since the centre of attention is the teacher viewed through the learning experiences and behaviour of a pupil. The pupil in question can be chosen at random, though for a better spread of information the approach works best in conjunction with the classroom activity/mobility mapping procedure. If you have already used this procedure, select at random two pupils from widely different groups identified by that method. If you have not used the classroom activity/mobility mapping procedure, read that section of this chapter and decide whether to do that first.

Whichever you decide, make sure that your chosen pupils are unaware of their role whilst the video recording of the lesson is being made.

Having chosen the two pupils for close observation, the procedure is simple but demands full concentration. You require two copies of the pupil pursuit record sheet on page 97, and a video recording of one of your lessons. Using the pupil pursuit record sheets, write the initials of the pupils at the top of the sheets. Start the video recording of the lesson from the beginning and record a brief comment on each pupil's specific activity to describe how he or she changes, noting the time at which any new activities started.

When you have completed the recording sheet for the whole lesson, read through your two sequences of comments carefully, looking for any patterns and indications of similarity or difference. Then go through each pupil's sequence individually adding a tick in the on-task box for

TYPES OF CLASSROOM TALK RECORD SHEET

Name of class/teaching group ___3 MN___ date ___4th Oct.___

TEACHER TALK

		TOTAL
Introducing work	✓✓✓✓✓	6
Giving instruction	✓✓✓	3
Exerting control	✓✓✓✓✓✓✓✓✓	10
Questioning	✓✓✓	3
Gaining attention	✓✓✓✓✓	6
Giving information	✓✓✓✓✓	6
Intervening between pupils	✓✓✓✓✓	5
Waiting / giving out books / checking (W) (B) (C)	W W W B B B C C C C C	11

PUPIL TALK

		TOTAL
Questioning teacher	✓✓✓✓✓	5
Pupil/pupil on-task talk	✓✓✓✓✓✓✓	7
Pupil/pupil off-task talk	✓✓✓✓✓	5
Answering teacher	✓✓✓✓	4
Pupil informing class		

	PUPIL PURSUIT RECORD SHEET	
	Name of class teaching group_____ date _____	
TIME	ACTIVITY	

each period that the pupil was on-task. Repeat the procedure for the second pupil.

- What is the overall level of both pupils' on-task performance?
- Is this level acceptable to you?

- Does it differ in any way from what you had expected?
- What differences are there between the two pupils' on-task levels?
- Are the differences acceptable and how do you account for them?
- What could you have done to improve the pupils on-task level?

PUPIL PURSUIT RECORD SHEET   pupil DE
Name of class teaching group __3 MN__ date 4th Oct

TIME	ACTIVITY
2.50	arrives late for lesson but first to arrive.
3.00	reading book seated at desk at back of class.
5.10	still reading book in secret, not attentive to teacher
9.00	shows interest in books being given out.
9.15	returned to reading story book in secret
16.10	now starts to listen to teacher
19.10	asks question and gets response from teacher, remains attentive
24.30	starts reading story book again in secret
25.50	sees teacher approaching, hides book and works to task
26.00	teacher checking work. asks question and gets answer
26.45	returns to story book as teacher moves away.
32.00	listens to teacher attentively talking at front of class
34.10	working to task set by teacher, continues working
43.05	distracted by pupil C's illness
44.15	watching teacher dealing with pupils A and B
47.20	listening to teacher
48.40	return to story book, reading in secret
57.15	puts story book away, listening to teacher
60.	leaves classroom with rest of pupils.

- How does their overall on-task level compare with your general impression of the on-task level of the whole class?

Looking back at your comments:

- What are your most frequent remarks?

TIME	ACTIVITY
PUPIL PURSUIT RECORD SHEET pupil DL	
Name of class teaching group __3MN__ date __4th Oct__	
3.15	Arrives late for lesson. One of first to arrive.
3.30	Sorting out books
4.00	Listening attentively to teacher
9.15	Checking book received from teacher
10.05	Talking quietly to neighbour
11.00	watching teacher deal with A and B
14.00	Listening to teacher
19.10	Questioning teacher / listening to teacher's answer
20.50	Listening carefully. full attention on teacher
23.10	working independently on set task
30.40	checking something with neighbour
31.00	Listening to teacher
35.00	working independently again
42.00	neighbour unwell, concerned
45.00	leave room with C to visit medical room.
	Does not return to class

- Does this pattern of remarks surprise you in any way?
- How might you expect it to be better or different?

The previous examples relate to the lesson recorded in detail in the classroom activity/mobility mapping sheet shown earlier. The times are recorded in minutes and seconds from the start of the lesson time. As can be seen the two pupils had completely different experiences in the lesson. Both appear to be working well. They are quiet and often attentive. But pupil DE is in fact not on-task and the teacher who makes a close contact only once remains ignorant of her secret reading.

Pupil pursuit using a video allows a very detailed insight into the work of a class. It also uncovers much of pupils' unseen behaviour. It is important that these insights are used to develop effective working practices but should not be used as a basis for disciplining pupils. The procedure is intended to give insight to teacher performance and, if this uncovers inadequate teacher awareness, pupils should not suffer as a result.

Time line records

This procedure represents a wide range of related activities that work very well with video-recorded lessons but can work equally well based upon personal recall, provided this is carried out immediately after the lesson. Because all the methods require you to make judgements on the quality of your own performance their value is only fully realised when the judgements are set against statements of objectives and intended outcomes. As a result the procedures can be time-consuming, but the quality of insight gained is well worth the effort.

a) Single lesson time line (V)

Choose a lesson or session at a time when you will have an opportunity to reflect on the quality of your work as soon as the lesson/activity is finished. The times just before lunch or at the end of the afternoon session are ideal.

You will need a copy of the single lesson time line recording sheet provided on page 101.

Allow yourself 30 minutes at the start of the day to complete the first section of the recording sheet. List the objectives and intended outcomes in their sub-sections and add any notes about the pupils, room, lesson content, proposed teaching methods, etc in the space provided.

The example below shows what a completed first section of the sheet may look like.

SINGLE LESSON TIME LINE RECORD SHEET

Name of class/teaching group _____ date _____

BEFORE THE LESSON

Objectives :

Planned outcomes:

Particular notes/Points for attention :

A ┤─ ─ ─ ─ ─ ─ ─ ─ ─ ─ ─ ─ ─

B ┤─ ─ ─ ─ ─ ─ ─ ─ ─ ─ ─ ─ ─

C ├─0─┼─5─┼─10─┼─15─┼─20─┼─25─┼─30─┼─35─┼─40─┼─45─┼─50─┼─55─┼─60─┤

D ┤─ ─ ─ ─ ─ ─ ─ ─ ─ ─ ─ ─ ─

E ┤─ ─ ─ ─ ─ ─ ─ ─ ─ ─ ─ ─ ─

SINGLE LESSON TIME LINE RECORD SHEET

Name of class/teaching group _____ date ____

BEFORE THE LESSON

Objectives : Distribute books and materials in orderly manner. Describe set tasks and organise pupils' work in pairs Complete written tasks. Control pupils A and B effectively

Planned outcomes : Each pupil will have completed ten assignments in pairs . and answered set questions. Pupils will be able to describe three basic fact about expansion A and B to complete same tasks.

Particular notes/Points for attention : Insufficient desks for all pupils, five need to sit facing windows at back of classroom. Need to reinforce control over A and B.

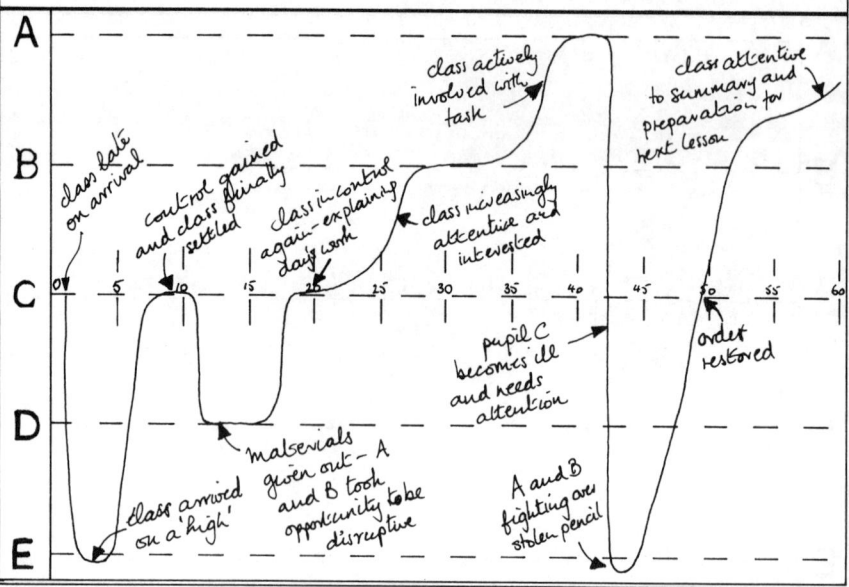

Drawing the time line

The time line grid covers one hour of recorded activity broken up into five-minute intervals along the horizontal axis. The vertical axis carries five levels of effectiveness defined as follows:

A = excellent effective work, objectives and intended outcomes are being achieved.

B = good effective work, most objectives and intended outcomes are being achieved.

C = reasonable work, some objectives and intended outcomes are being achieved.

D = not effective enough, few objectives and intended outcomes are being achieved.

E = ineffective work, none of the objectives and intended outcomes is being achieved.

Immediately after the lesson, if you are not working from a video recording, analyse your work in terms of the five levels of effectiveness described above. Better still, play back your video recording and judge the effectiveness level as you watch it. On the basis of your observation draw a line to represent the level of effectiveness against time showing the peaks of good quality and the troughs when things did not go well.

Clearly this procedure is not a precise and accurate tool but it does allow for the creation of overall patterns and impressions.

The example on page 102 illustrates the kind of fluctuations that can arise, many of which are unexpected but a normal part of everyday teaching. The lesson line is based upon the detailed record included earlier on the classroom activity/mobility mapping sheet.

The activity in this simple form can be very useful as a source of reflection on the lesson/activity. The following prompts which relate to the recorded lesson are the kind needed to stimulate the process.

- How could I have dealt with the class's late arrival to reduce the negative effect?
- What was it about my presentation of information that held the class's attention?
- What was it about the set task that raised and maintained pupils' on-task level?
- How could I have prevented the fight between A and B?
- Did pupil C show any signs of being ill on arrival in class?
- Do I know the school's current procedures for dealing with sick pupils?
- What was it about my treatment of A and B that allowed class activity to be regained so quickly?

- What was it about my end-of-lesson summary that caused the class to leave on such a positive note?

If it is possible to complete your time line based upon a video recording of the lesson, this will give you not only more precise time references for specific developments in the lesson but also allow you to do multiple lines on the one chart. For example, you may decide to focus on very precise aspects of your work: your use of voice; your movements around the classroom; the level of class noise; your quality of class control. The same approach can be used with the pupil pursuit procedure to record individual pupil 'performance' and in this way if the records are kept for comparison with later records a view of 'productivity' and development is achievable.

b) Day's time line (V)

This procedure is a very comprehensive approach to recording personal performance. It takes time and effort to complete, and requires a high level of personal commitment and good organisational skills. However, if maintained it will provide you with very detailed information on which to base your self-appraisal of classroom teaching. As with the single lesson time line, the value of the work is only fully realised when the judgement of performance is based upon prestated objectives and intended outcomes. If the approach seems like a return to your days of teaching practice as a student, do not be put off by that. Your knowledge of the quality of your classroom teaching is a key part of your required appraisal review. You need a clear view of the quality of your work and the evidence for this based upon a range of systematic approaches and procedures. Working in this way you are in a better position to describe your work, your strengths and limitations, and to describe your related professional development needs. The procedure is strengthened even more if you can find a partner with whom you can work, so that you may assist each other to keep to task and thoroughly reflect on the day's work.

For this procedure you will need a copy of the following recording sheets:

1 Day's time line — overview/planning sheet
2 Day's time line — record sheet
3 Day's time line — action sheet

Decide at least one week in advance when you intend to start keeping your day's time line record. Recognise the effort it will take and try to recruit a partner with whom you will work. Set aside one hour for your initial discussions and preparations, and assume that you will need a further hour together at the end, and 30 minutes at the start, on the

DAY'S TIME LINE   OVERVIEW/PLANNING SHEET
Name of class/teaching group _____ date _____
PRE-REGISTRATION SESSION
REGISTRATION/ASSEMBLY
SESSION 1
SESSION 2
LUNCH BREAK
SESSION 3
SESSION 4
AFTER-SCHOOL SESSION

DAY'S TIME LINE RECORD SHEET

Name of class / teaching group _____   date _____

	session 1	session 2	session 3	session 4
A				
B				
C				
D				
E				

```
┌─────────────────────────────────────────────────────┐
│  DAY'S TIME LINE ACTION SHEET                         │
├─────────────────────────────────────────────────────┤
│  Name of class / teaching group _____ date _____   │
├─────────────────────────────────────────────────────┤
│  My skills and knowledge in which I have confidence  │
│  are:                                                 │
│                                                       │
├─────────────────────────────────────────────────────┤
│  The skills and knowledge I need to develop further  │
│  are:                                                 │
│                                                       │
├─────────────────────────────────────────────────────┤
│  The training I need for this development is:         │
│                                                       │
│                                                       │
├─────────────────────────────────────────────────────┤
│  The person/people with whom I need to discuss this  │
│  is/are:                                              │
│                                                       │
├─────────────────────────────────────────────────────┤
│  I will ask for a meeting on:                         │
│                                                       │
├─────────────────────────────────────────────────────┤
│  My intended outcomes for this meeting are:           │
│                                                       │
│                                                       │
└─────────────────────────────────────────────────────┘
```

day that you do the main work. Agree the times and place of these meetings. Having decided (and hopefully agreed with a partner) the day for your task, complete the overview/planning sheet to set out your objectives and intended outcomes.

Planning the day in full detail is essential for completion of the task. Also, because it will take every spare moment in the day, make sure that the senior staff are aware of what you are doing so that they do not call on you for additional duties on the day. Better still, discuss the task with the headteacher so she or he knows how professional you are in your contribution to the performance appraisal process.

Concentrate on each section of the planning sheet separately. Write out your precise objectives, intended outcomes and any other particular notes or points for attention. You may choose to focus on just one or two objectives and outcomes in each session, perhaps keeping the same ones throughout the day if this is appropriate to your current needs. Or you may choose a wide spread covering many aspects of your work with variations from session to session. It is entirely your choice. The two examples on pages 108 and 109 illustrate the kind of tasks which may be selected.

If you do not have responsibility for class registration leave this section blank.

DAY'S TIME LINE   OVERVIEW/PLANNING SHEET

Name of class/teaching group 1st year Juniors date 4 Oct

PRE-REGISTRATION SESSION

meet partner to discuss day's planned work.
check partner's reactions and her planning for the day.
remind each other of afterschool meeting. Remind head of our plans.

REGISTRATION/ASSEMBLY

Register class and attend assembly. Collect video for session 2.

SESSION 1
Remind class of previous work on homes by reference to the displayed planner sheet. Introduce ideas of home design. Features of different houses and their need to withstand extreme weather. Give out magazines with home plans. Working in groups list materials used in home construction and the types of rooms in peoples' homes. Check each group

SESSION 2
Hand out plain paper for designs, cardboard, scissors, glue for construction. Group task: design and make a house that would be able to withstand high winds. Show video of recent news coverage of tornado action. Pupils to work individually but sharing construction materials. Explain about testing conditions to follow. Why test?

LUNCH BREAK
Return video to Mrs N Complete time lines from morning sessions. Check hair drier for afternoon session and stand and clamp to hold it. Collect stopwatch from Mr S.

SESSION 3
Complete constructions and produce drawings of the houses with accurate measurements recorded on the sheets. Hand out house design sheets for each pupil to complete. Describe testing arrangements using a hair drier to simulate high winds. Explain and discuss how the testing can be standardised and the need to record time in the tests. Agree the test procedure.

SESSION 4
Test model houses and display results as bar chart on wall display. Class to write a description of their constructions and the testing arrangements. Each pupil to suggest three ways in which their design and construction could be improved

AFTER-SCHOOL SESSION

Complete afternoon sessions time lines. Explain record to partner and listen to the explanation of their record. Identify good and bad aspects of the work. Agree changes for next session with class. Discuss whether this paired working for self appraisal is worthwhile.

DAY'S TIME LINE OVERVIEW/PLANNING SHEET

date 4ᵗʰ Oct

PRE-REGISTRATION SESSION

go over details of lesson, check materials and equipment. See headteacher, remind her of agreement not to include me in cover arrangements

REGISTRATION/ASSEMBLY

Register tutor group. final check on plans for morning's lessons.

SESSION 1   1ˢᵗ year combined science: Materials. Working in threes, pupils to experience whole range of available materials to identify similarities and differences. Use odd one out game to reinforce idea of properties of materials. All pupils to complete assignment sheet 4. Check that all pupils are actively involved.

SESSION 2   5ᵗʰ year GCSE Biology: Structure of the Human Eye. Go over previous work, use models of the eye to reinforce information on structure and functions. Hand out 20 basic facts sheets. Use initial factual recall test to conclude work on the eye. Hand out information sheets on the human ear.

LUNCH BREAK

Fill in time lines for morning session
Help technician to set up expansion materials for 3ʳᵈ year

SESSION 3 3ʳᵈ year low ability group: Expansion. Circus arrangement of investigation in pairs. Ten sets of equipment with illustrated instruction cards. Give out recording sheets. Pairs to complete a single record of their combined work. Check on 3 basic facts about expansion.

SESSION 4 6ᵗʰ form tutorial session: A level Biology Go over assignment 5 with JN and CB. Check progress on assignment reports for whole group. Remind DL of interview dates and deadlines for applications. Discuss work problems with VN and possible alternative courses.

AFTER-SCHOOL SESSION

Fill in time lines for afternoon sessions
meet DK to compare work and discuss time lines

Day's time line — record sheet
As the two examples show, both teachers intended to complete their time lines for the morning during the mid-day break. We recommend you to do this since it is difficult to carry details over to the end of the day. This record sheet has the same five levels of performance as used on the single lesson time line sheet. The criteria for the five levels A to E are as described earlier.

Completing the time line
Consider the actual outcomes of each lesson carefully, comparing these with the planned objectives and intended outcomes. Try to represent all the stages in the development of the lesson, adding notes to describe the events at points along the line. As you draw in the line, keep a close eye on the time base in order to keep the sequence of events correctly placed. If you decided on only one or two very precise objectives, try representing their outcomes as separate lines using different colours for each objective. If you are able to video record your lessons, this will allow you to plot your time line with more precision and to gain greater insight into the quality of your work as you review it.

When you have completed your time lines for the day's sessions discuss these with your partner. Use the following prompts to structure your reflection/discussion.

- What pleased me most about each session was . . .
- What disappointed me most about each session was . . .
- What surprised me most about each session was . . .
- The main things I learned from this experience are. . .
- If I were doing this again I would . . .
- When I was most successful it was because . . .
- When I was least successful it was because . . .
- The main differences between the sessions were . . .

Finally, when you have fully reflected on your work, complete the day's time line action sheet as a record of your future intentions. This should be completed in consultation with your partner if you have one, or, if you have not, make arrangements to discuss what you have been doing, and your future intentions, with the headteacher or another senior member of staff.

The day's time line procedure has a number of strengths. As well as allowing you to gain greater insight into your personal skills and abilities, it sharpens your awareness of weaknesses so that you can describe them precisely as a basis for your future in-service training needs and allows you to be more confident of your strengths so that these too can be described.

The following examples of day's time lines match the examples of

DAY'S TIME LINE RECORD SHEET

Name of class / teaching group 1st year junior class   date 4th Oct

	Session 1	Session 2	Session 3	Session 4
A				
B	pupils well motivated by tasks but not very clear	television news really clarifies need for sound construction	whole class working very well — discussion of testing arrangements too slow	testing went very well and collection of times very useful as basis for comparing designs and construction — written work very good
C	quite a good start	insufficient magazines and other materials, some pupils becoming restless and disruptive — distribution of construction materials raises level of enthusiasm and effort.	class wanting to get on with it	
D				
E				

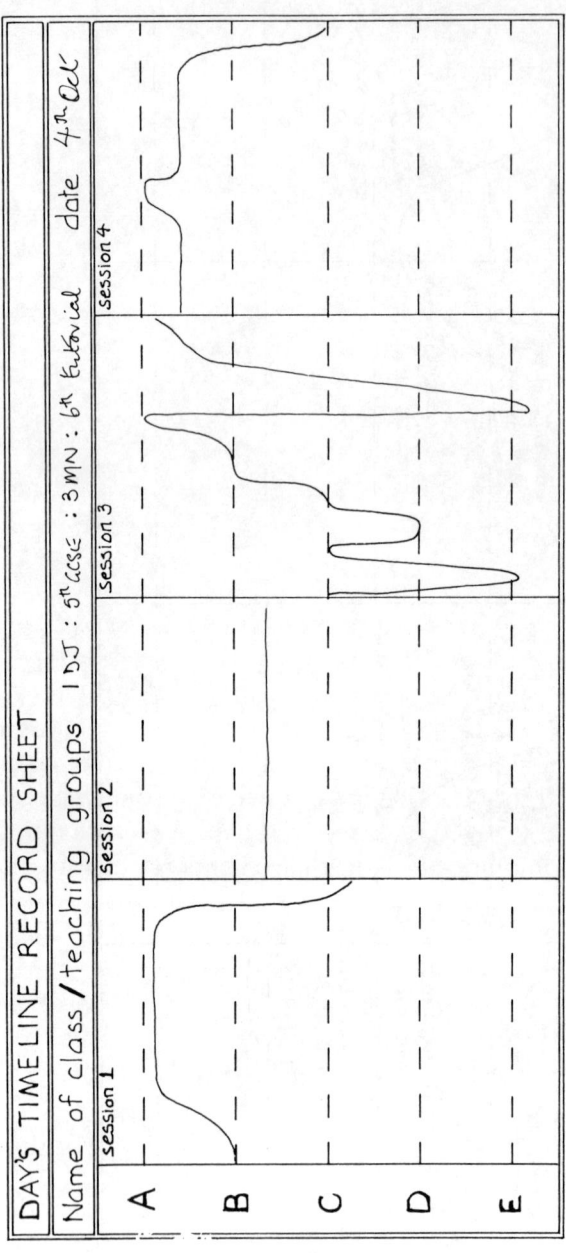

DAY'S TIME LINE RECORD SHEET

Name of class / teaching groups 1 DJ : 5ᵗʰ GCSE : 3MN : 6ᵗʰ Tutorial   date 4ᵗʰ Oct

Session 1   Session 2   Session 3   Session 4

A B C D E

Session 1 not all materials ready for start of lesson, everyone worked well but insufficient time to round off the lesson and complete assignment sheets, hence dip in line.

Session 2 well motivated group but uninspired lesson. Needs greater practical input. Probably need to return to direction of eye again

Session 3 See more detailed explanation on sheet 'single lesson Time Line Record Sheet'

Session 4 very good lesson until counselling VN went badly wrong. Need to follow this up urgently.

overview/planning sheets provided earlier. The pattern of lines for the secondary teacher reflects the changing nature of secondary teaching, whereas the primary teacher working with a single class is able to produce a developing single-line record of the day's work.

Pupil perceptions/client concerns

In the pressure of the day-to-day delivery of teaching and learning it is too easy to forget that the purpose of the teaching process is to support the growth and development of learners. Learners are teachers' clients and the effects which go into teaching are to serve clients' needs. In secondary schools in particular it is sometimes easy to lose sight of this teacher/client relationship. At its worst, subjects themselves become the clients with public examinations working as the vehicles for serving their needs. In the crush to complete the syllabus or fulfil the scheme of work the learner as client is too easily lost.

Similarly, the needs of learners can become secondary when a teacher's preoccupation is the determined need to retain the subject within the curriculum at all cost. Here, the primary motivation seldom puts the learners/clients at the centre of attention. Instead it is often personal principles or academic traditions that are articulated to defend hallowed ground. The pupils' place in this debate is purely by association: if teacher says it is good then it must be good for the pupil.

If a primary aim of education is to help learners to achieve sufficient knowledge, experience and skills critically to consider their circumstances in life then there seems little point in retaining curriculum contact merely to keep traditions alive. Therefore, if learners are teachers' clients it is essential that teachers communicate with their clients to identify and work to their needs and gain a view of their perceptions of the teaching/learning process. In so far as pupils are the only people in schools who experience the whole school, moving from class to class in primary schools and from teacher to teacher in secondary schools, it is bordering on crass incompetence that we have not developed systems for regularly receiving their feedback on the quality of teaching and learning. This activity is one way in which the error can be corrected.

The procedure uses sampling interviews to collect information from pupils. It is a continuous process relying on the accumulation of views over a period of time. The assumptions which lie behind it are: that teachers have the skills to question pupils in ways which will draw out accurate and honest information; that pupils have clear insights and feelings about the quality of their learning experiences and teacher's skills and abilities; that pupils can accurately articulate their views and will do so when they understand the underlying purpose; and that if the

PUPIL PERCEPTIONS/CLIENT CONCERNS RECORD SHEET
Name of class/teaching group _____ pupil ___ date _____
Q1
Q2
Q3
Q4
Q5
Q6
Q7
Q8
Q9
Q10

PUPIL PERCEPTIONS/CLIENT CONCERNS RECORD SHEET

Name of class/teaching group _____ pupil ____ date _____

Q1 Tell me what you think I wanted you to learn in the last lesson.

Q2 What do you think you learnt in the last lesson?

Q3 Did you find anything difficult in the last lesson? If so, what was it?

Q4 Did you particularly enjoy any parts of the last lesson? If so, which parts?

Q5 Were there any parts you didn't enjoy at all? If so, which parts?

Q6 When I am explaining things in class, would you say my explanations were:
Very clear? ☐ clear? ☐ mainly clear? ☐ not very clear? ☐
very unclear? ☐

Q7 When we use work sheets that I have produced would you describe them as:
Very clear? ☐ clear? ☐ mainly clear? ☐ not very clear? ☐
very unclear? ☐

Q8 How would you describe the level of difficulty of the work I set for you?
very easy ☐ quite easy ☐ just right ☐ quite hard ☐ very hard ☐

Q9 Is there anything else you would like to say?

procedure is conducted in a manner which clearly values pupils' views it will help to build even better teacher/pupil classroom relationships.

The pupil perception/client concerns record sheet is provided for recording pupils' responses. The questions are only examples of the kind you may choose to use. Certainly the questions need to relate directly to the lesson or activity that has just concluded. The critical aspect of the procedure is the style and skill with which the questions are put and the answer received. There must be no hint of pressure, stress or coercion in the questioning, or negative response in receiving the answers or the procedure has no purpose. The pupil must be relaxed and secure for you to be able to get the best information.

How many pupils should be interviewed?

This is very much determined by the circumstances at the time of the interviews and the age of the interviewees. Clearly the interviews need to be brief, especially with young pupils when the questions will be more simple and straightforward. Even so they take time, and pupils cannot be expected to wait long before it is their turn, especially if it is in their own time. Our recommendation is a maximum of three at one time if the interviews are intended to be brief, and a maximum of two at one time if the interviews are more extensive.

Identifying the pupils

Pupils must be randomly identified if a valid picture is to be built up. This can be achieved in a number of arbitrary ways: every ninth pupil through the door at the start of the session or asking the form tutor to choose three names at random from the class register are two possibilities.

When should the interviews be carried out?

The interviews must take place immediately at the end of a lesson or session. Ideal times are at morning or afternoon breaks. Lunchtimes and after-school periods are possibilities but there are many other calls on time which must be taken into account. Whatever time you choose do not forget to make it clear that there is no compulsion and, for example, if there is a need to visit the toilet or see someone else first this is quite acceptable. The pupils are doing you the favour!

Where should the interview take place?

In the most comfortable and least threatening situation for the pupils. Ideally away from the classroom and on 'neutral' territory. If the school has a waiting area for visitors then this is ideal.

What should be said to the pupils?

It is very important to explain the purpose of the interview clearly and to stress that the pupil's help is being sought. The pupil must also know that it is only by chance that he or she is being asked to do it and that he or she can say no and there will be no bad reactions to this. The following statement is offered as an example of the type that should be used on *all* occasions.

> Thanks for staying behind at the end of the lesson. I am hoping that you will help me with some work that I am doing. I want to know how my pupils feel about my teaching and I will be interviewing a number of pupils over the next few weeks to ask their views. You were chosen purely at random. There is no secret reason why I am asking you, and you do not need to do it if you do not want to. I will think no less of you if you say no.
>
> If you agree I will ask you 'N' questions and record your answers on this sheet. I will check what I have written with you to make sure it is accurate. It should not take us more than about ten minutes at the most. Will you do it?

Conduct of the interview

The questions must relate only to the lesson about which you are collecting information. It is not reasonable to expect pupils to give a view on contact made days or weeks before. Give each question directly to the pupil and be very patient if a response is slow in coming. In the early days, before 'word gets around', pupils may be uncertain and will need time to sort out the differences between how they feel about the process and the answers they are clarifying in their own minds.

Do not repeat the question or prompt the pupil unless you have waited so long that the pupil is coming under stress. Do not repeat the question because you cannot cope with the silence. Some of the questions are paired, the first question is closed, to gain a simple YES or NO answer, as a stem to an associated open question. This is a more helpful way to prompt more detailed information.

Checking out the answers

When you have collected all the answers that the pupil is willing to offer, check the responses by feeding back the information in the form of a paraphrase. For example consider the following recorded responses:

> I could not see any single purpose to the lesson. I suppose you wanted us to do the work you set us.
>
> I think I learnt the names of the part of the eye, at least some of them, and what their functions are.

No I did not find any difficulties.

I did not enjoy any particular part of the lesson, it was all right.

Your explanations are mainly clear.

Your work materials are very clear.

The lessons are very easy.

I like the subject and want to study it further.

The feedback to this pupil might be:

Thank you for your answer. Let me check my information. You said that you could not see any single purpose to the lesson, you supposed that I wanted you to do the work set. [Pause — to check reaction.] You did not find the lesson difficult nor did you enjoy any particular part of the lesson. It was all right. [Pause — to check reaction.] You think my explanations in class are mainly clear, the lesson was easy and you like the subject and intend to study it further. [Pause — to check reaction.]

Thank you for your responses they are very helpful to me. I will be asking more of your class to help me in future. I may ask you again.

Using the responses

The individual responses from pupils are helpful in themselves since they enrich the teacher's view of the pupils and contribute to better teacher/pupil understanding and relationships. However, it is the accumulating view which is most helpful since it gives a broader perspective of pupils' reactions and feelings. It is also possible through the prolonged use of this approach to gauge the effects of introduced changes in teaching styles, pace or content.

This approach is a valuable method of gaining information over time. It can be further developed so that many more pupils can be involved and in the next procedure this is explained.

Prompts for reflection

- How well do your pupils cope with this request?
- How detailed are their responses?
- What is your impression of their feelings about this approach?
- How do their responses match your expectations or assumptions about their responses?
- What actions do you intend to take based on this information?

Group perceptions/client concerns

This approach builds upon the work of the preceding activity though it is not necessary to use the previous approach before adopting this one. Ideally the two should be used together so that the benefits of a one-to-one contact can be balanced with a wider range of responses, each introduced as a normal and integral part of teacher/pupil working relationships.

In this procedure the whole class is actively involved in the process which should be introduced on a regular basis to sample pupils' attitudes and opinions and as a way of checking the outcomes of particular pieces of work, eg themes or topics.

The process involves providing pupils with prompt booklets to guide structured conversations in pairs. The booklets also double up as a recording device. The booklets are designed so that the same question is posed to each member of a pair and space is provided on the opposite page of the booklet for the responses. The pages have a letter and number code. The letters relate to the pupils and the numbers relate to the questions.

The prompt booklets

A blank master sheet for photocopying and one example of a prompt booklet ready for construction are included in this section. The booklets consist of centre-folded sheets produced by cutting full sheets in half down the middle line of each page. The sheets are best held together by a single centre staple on the fold.

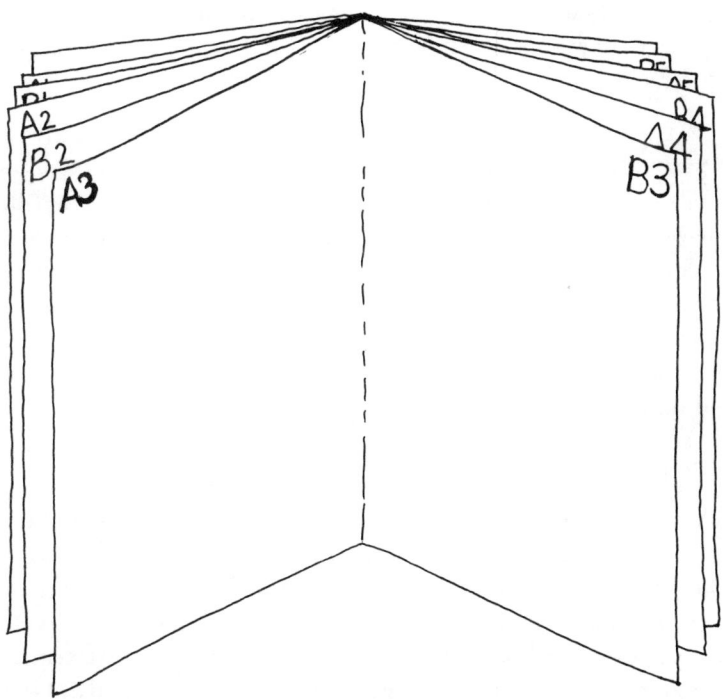

Note that, as in the case illustrated above, an odd number of sheets is needed in each booklet if the layout is to be achieved without back-to-back printing. Also the centre sheet always carries both the A and the B questions unlike the other sheets. The outer cover is obtained from the other half of the centre sheet. See the full set of sheets and the instructions for construction on p. 122.

How many pupils should be involved?

This procedure uses the whole class which should first be organised into working pairs. Within each pair one pupil chooses to be pupil A and the other becomes pupil B.

How are the booklets to be used?

Explain the use of the booklets and their purpose as follows:

> I am very interested to know your views about my teaching and what you have been learning. I need your help to give me information about what you have learnt and your feelings about the work.

> I want each of you to work with a partner. When you have decided on your partner get into pairs and agree who will be pupil A and who will be B.

Give one booklet to each pair.

> You will see that on each page there is either an A question or a B question. All questions are in pairs so you all get the same chance to give your opinions.

> Pupil A is the first to answer question 1. Pupil B's job is to write down their partner's answer opposite question A1. The booklet is then passed to pupil A who asks question B1 of his or her partner and writes down the answer on the page opposite question B1. The booklet is passed back to B who asks A question A2 and so on until all the questions have been asked and all the answers recorded. I will collect your completed booklets at the end of the session. I will also keep an eye on your rate of progress and remind you when you should be half way through. The whole exercise should only take about ten minutes.

Using the responses

The group perceptions/clients' concerns record sheet provides a way of scoring pupil responses. For each question decide the kind of comments that you judge to be supportive and positive, those that are neutral or non-committal, and those that are critical and negative. Go through the set of prompt booklets and tick one of the boxes in the appropriate sections against each question. Note that nil returns must also be scored.

GROUP PERCEPTIONS / CLIENTS' CONCERNS RECORD SHEET

Name of class/teaching group _____   date _____

QUESTION	Supportive/positive response	neutral response	critical/negative response	no response
1				
2				
3				
4				
5				
6				
7				
8				

TOTALS	supportive/positive	neutral	critical/negative	no response

By totalling the scores in each section you will gain a view of the pattern of responses to individual items and the overall pattern of group response.

This procedure can form an effective part of your normal working routine by building it into the final session of each topic or sequence of lessons related to a specific part of your scheme of work. In the light of the National Curriculum assessment arrangements it is a helpful way of gaining an overview of a group's perceptions of their teaching/learning in relation to their emerging pattern of attainments.

Making a group response booklet

Photocopy the necessary number of blank master sheets. You will always need one cover sheet/centre page question sheet and the necessary number of question sheets to make up the rest of the booklet.

Write out the questions in your chosen sequence making sure that the same question appears in each matched pair, ie A1 B1, A2 B2 etc. Photocopy these master sheets to produce enough prompt booklets for the class (half the number of pupils in the group). When the copies are completed cut each sheet across the centre dotted line and collate the half sheets into booklet sets as shown. Fold each set down the middle.

Please note that you can make the booklets as long or as short as you

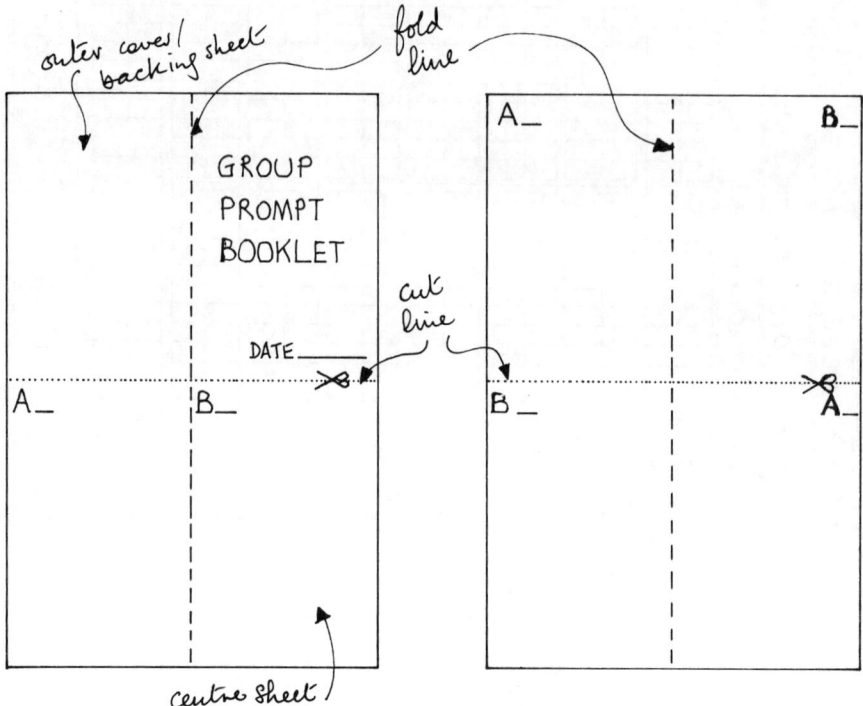

like and when you first use the approach you will find that short booklets are needed to make it easier for the pupils to become familiar with the way of working.

NB   This teachnique has many possible applications. It is a ready vehicle for pupil self-assessment and can be used with experienced users of the approach to create pupils' own prompt booklets, giving rise to far greater insight into pupils' understanding, attitudes and responses.

Prompts for reflection

- What is the overall pattern of response from your classes?
- Which, if any, of the responses have proved to be a surprise?

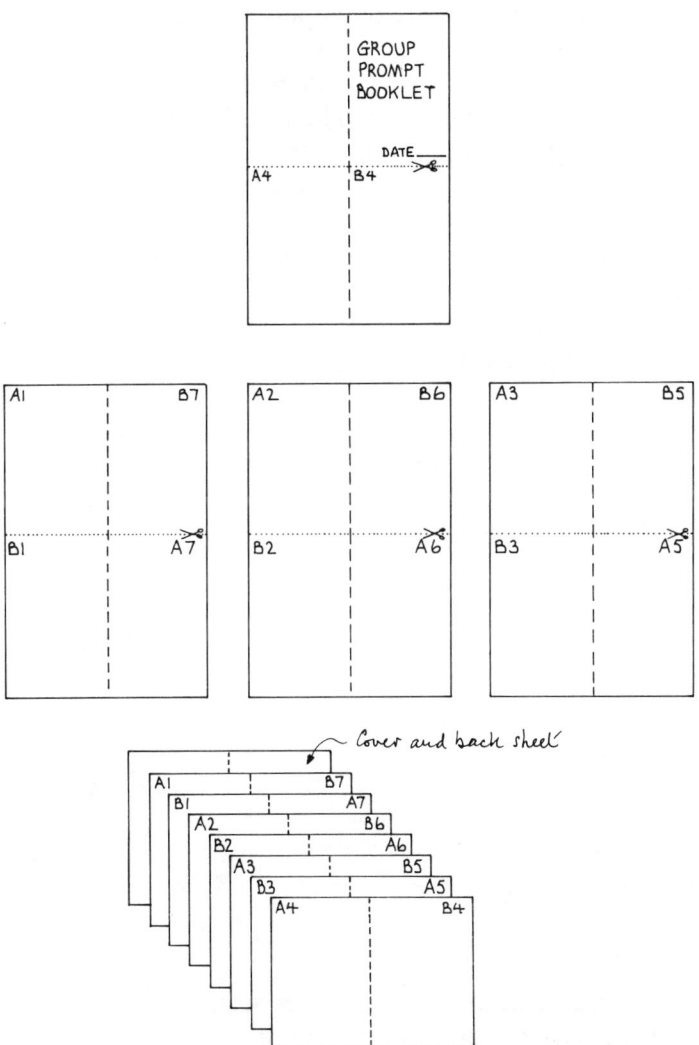

- What actions do you intend to take now that you have this more detailed information from your classes?
- With whom do you intend to discuss this information?

Course work marking review

If the school has a policy which sets store by pupils' course work whether this is done in class or at home then there must be a very good quality of response in teacher's marking. Too often in HMI reports reference is made to inadequate marking restricted to ticks on pages, scores out of a total, a single letter or number score at the end of a piece of work and/ or a single word or short phrase comment. If marking is restricted in this way it provides no feedback for pupils about the overall impressions of the work or value judgements about performance in relation to degree of difficulty of the task or expected performance. Neither does it engage the pupil in any form of on-going dialogue with the teacher about the purpose or standard of the work. The positive impact on pupils of a range of personal comments from the teacher, both positive and negative, can be quite marked and significantly raise levels of pupils expectations of their own performance and commitment to the work in hand.

This procedure is, therefore, entirely retrospective in its application and is used to identify a level of past and existing performance as a basis for judging the overall quality of this aspect of your work. The list on the course work/homework marking sheet gives examples of the kind of marking found in books.

It is not intended to be definitive and you may wish to extend it to include specific approaches to marking that you have developed.

Use of the procedure

Choose four sets of books from quite different groups that you have taught for some time. Take ten books at random from each pile of books. Choose two pieces of work from each set of books and note their dates on the record sheet provided.

Go through the chosen pieces of work for each of the two dates in the four sets of books and place a tick for each piece of work in the appropriate boxes against the different statements describing the marking provided.

After completing the four sets of books total up the scores against each statement to gain an overall view.

Prompts for reflection

- Is there a single pattern across all four sets?
- How do the patterns differ between sets?

COURSE WORK/HOMEWORK MARKING REVIEW RECORD SHEET   date _____

	class/teaching group 1 dates:	class/teaching group 2 dates:	class/teaching group 3 dates:	class/teaching group 4 dates:
Total absence of marks or comments	☐	☐	☐	☐
Ticks against parts of the work no other comments	☐	☐	☐	☐
Ticks against parts of the work plus single score or letter grade	☐	☐	☐	☐
Single score or letter grade no other marking	☐	☐	☐	☐
Correction of spelling, grammar and/or punctuation	☐	☐	☐	☐
Factual corrections without explanations	☐	☐	☐	☐
Factual correction with explanation	☐	☐	☐	☐
Personal comments directed at the work	☐	☐	☐	☐
Personal comments directed at the pupil	☐	☐	☐	☐
Additional questions for repetition of work	☐	☐	☐	☐
Additional questions for extension of work	☐	☐	☐	☐
Reference sources provided to enrich work	☐	☐	☐	☐
Request to meet and discuss work	☐	☐	☐	☐

- What actions, if any, do you propose to take as a result of this survey of your approach to marking?

Professional stages

As all professionals develop in their chosen career they go through stages which characterise their state of readiness, confidence, understanding and capacity to fulfil their role. In the earliest days personal concerns often include the most superficial aspects of work as well as basic and fundamental needs. As time goes by, and experience and confidence grows, concerns can give way to self-satisfaction and even apathy, and the need to maintain personal and professional momentum and direction can be lost. There is also the danger that self-fulfilment can become more important than serving clients' needs, and in the teaching profession, along with other caring professions, this too can lead to loss of direction. Equally dangerous is the lure of professional progress at a pace that outstrips real experience where the momentum of current progress propels the individual into a role for which she or he is ill-prepared, even unable, to achieve success. We have identified these issues in a set of questions to prompt personal reflection. They are intended to be private questions, but they could equally be the basis of a professional conversation with a trusted colleague which could well have greater benefit.

   As you work your way through the list of questions, highlight those that 'ring a bell' with you; and having been through all the prompts once, go back to those you have highlighted for further attention.

   1 Am I concerned about the way I am dressed in school?
   2 Am I anxious about getting to school on time?
   3 Am I anxious about being in the right place at the right time?
   4 Am I concerned each time I have to meet a new class?
   5 Do I know the names of most of the pupils I teach?
   6 Do I know my timetable well?
   7 Do I know the syllabuses and schemes of work I am using?
   8 Do I know the school policies?
   9 Do I know the LEA policies?
   10 Do I know the National Curriculum to which I am working?
   11 How confident do I feel about my classroom organisation?
   12 How confident do I feel about my classroom control?
   13 How confident do I feel about my management of classroom learning experiences for pupils?
   14 To what extent am I clear about my own objectives in teaching?

15 To what extent am I able to relate my actual teaching to my personal objectives?
16 To what extent do I reflect on my personal performance as a teacher?
17 To what extent am I aware of my professional development needs?
18 To what extent am I aware of my pupils' home/family/community circumstances?
19 To what extent do I plan my teaching to match my pupils' needs?
20 To what extend am I aware of pupils' other learning experiences?
21 To what extent do I attempt to integrate the learning experiences I provide with those provided by other teachers?
22 To what extent do I take account of pupils' special learning needs?
23 To what extent am I aware of other teachers' work?
24 To what extent do I positively facilitate the transfer of pupils' learning from other teachers?
25 To what extent do I help pupils to transfer the lessons learnt with me to other settings?
26 To what extent am I preoccupied with my teaching at the expense of my pupils' learning needs?
27 How do I feel I am progressing as a teacher?
28 What are my next targets for professional development?
29 What is my next career step?
30 What is my career goal?
31 What contributions am I making to the general life of the school?
32 What contributions am I making to my peers?
33 How am I supporting the senior staff in school?
34 What is my image with the parents of the pupils I teach?
35 How do the governors feel about my work?

If you keep a personal record of your performance appraisals, and you should, then it will be helpful to you to keep a copy of the prompts in this section and the record of those items you highlighted. In a year's time look back at the list and see how you have changed.

Teaching practice report

We have all experienced teaching practice reports and wondered about their accuracy and reliability. Here is your chance to put them to the test by designing your own proforma. The procedure has two parts. In the first part you decide what key elements make up an effective teacher. Having decided on your list set each item as a heading in the teaching practice record sheet provided and then fill in the comments and award yourself grades for each section, and overall grades at the end, according to the criteria provided for you.

Deciding the key elements

Select from the following list and add your own items if you feel there are omissions.

- Knowledge of subject matter appropriate to pupils' needs
- Ability to design effective learning materials
- Classroom management
- Classroom control
- Contribution to general life of school
- Recording pupil attainment
- Reporting pupil attainment
- Lesson development
- Support for pupil progression of learning
- Relationships with school management
- Relationships with pupils
- Relationships with other teachers
- Relationships with parents
- Reliability to carry out commitments.

Write your chosen headings in the blank record proforma provided. Note the range of criteria for grading your performance and decide where you lie for each of the statements you make about yourself. Work through the record and describe your current performance against the headings. Add the individual grades then complete the boxes marked overall grade and future potential.

- Why did you choose the particular headings for your report?
- Which of the headings provided most difficulty in commenting on?
- Which of the headings represents your greatest strengths?
- Of the headings you excluded, do any represent a problem area requiring attention?

As with most of the other activities, this one is more effective when shared with a trusted colleague, especially if both partners fill in and share their report sheet records.

A variation of this basic procedure is to agree your own headings but to exchange report sheets with your partner and complete each other's. Clearly you need to know each other's work very well to do this effectively, but if you have used some of the other procedures in this chapter then this approach can represent a very satisfying culmination of productive mutual support.

Today's picture

This procedure is meant to be fun as well as an effective way of representing yourself and your feelings. You do not have to be a gifted

TEACHING PRACTICE RECORD SHEET

Performance report for period _____ to _____

The grades A to E are awarded according to these criteria:

A maintains a high standard

B generally good standard, room for improvement

C adequate, but lacks sustained quality

D inadequate. Need for considerable improvement

E unacceptable standard

overall grade □

future potential

| EXCELLENT | VERY GOOD | GOOD | FAIR | LIMITED |

artist to use it and you do not have to share your feelings with anyone else. Having said that, we have known teachers who have used this as a 'normal' part of their morning greeting for their class or tutor group. For them it became a way of communicating and showing their trust and relationship with young people. Needless to say it helped them considerably and also provided a good way for their pupils to communicate with them.

All you do is work as spontaneously as you can in simple illustrations to represent how you feel.

If you are part of a support group of staff try drawing a group picture.

Small ads

We are all familiar with the short advertisements used in newspapers and shop windows to attract a customer for a sale. This simple procedure uses the same idea. The purpose is to be brief, positive, and attractive in your self-description. But remember, the Trades Descriptions Act requires accurate information which can be demonstrated by fact!

The challenge is to write an advertisement to sell yourself in a postcard-sized space, describing your skills, knowledge, experience and other attributes using only thirty-five words. The trick is to decide on the keywords before building up your sentences.

Having written your small ad, decide the type of job for which you were advertising your services. Having decided on the post, write an advertisement for this job setting out the nature of the role, the key aspects of the tasks and line management responsibilities/lines of reporting. Now check your original small ad against the job advertisement you have just written. Would you be suitable for the post? How realistic is your small ad and the job advertisement you have produced?

Market stall

This activity is similar to small ads except that you are required to display your not-quite-so-good qualities as well as those which you see as your main attributes.

When applying for a new post, or later on in the interview process, it is always best to have a clear view of your strengths and weaknesses. To indicate the latter can be very positive especially if it is done in the

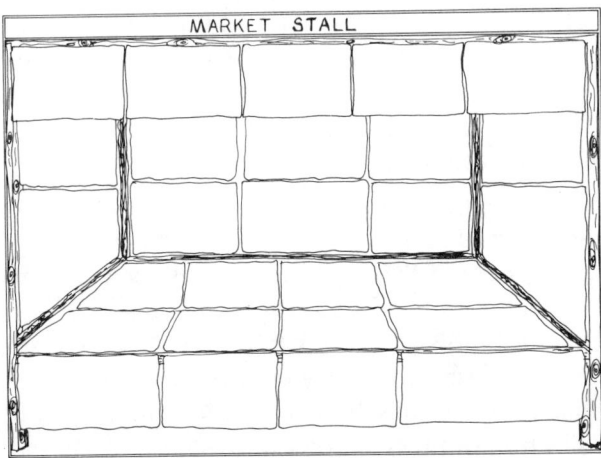

context of establishing a strong sense of self-awareness and a realistic expression of existing capabilities and knowledge of future needs. Many interviewers will feel positive about candidates with such self-awareness.

The activity is simple: fill in the spaces on the illustration of the market stall giving a single attribute or need for further development in each space. Remember, your customers will see the front of the stall first, so set out your best wares in this position. You must also think where best to display the things that still give you some concern.

What would you do if . . .?

This procedure is designed to allow you to test your skills, knowledge and experience in deciding how best to handle situations that may arise in your teaching. As with the other activities, this one is more productive if used with a partner. In this way you can check out each other's solutions and work out the feasibility of each.

Read each scenario carefully, identify the key facts and issues, then decide your range of options. From these options choose your best option.

Scenario 1: Class 3A is the top group of a ten-form-entry mixed comprehensive school. The groups are timetabled in two five-form sets. A girl, SH, has an excellent previous record of 1st and 2nd year work but for no apparent reason she is now producing completely unacceptable classwork and no homework. She has also changed her friendship pattern, and her behaviour is deteriorating.

Scenario 2: You are the form teacher of a second-year junior class of a one-form-entry junior and infant school. The class has twenty-three boys and only eight girls. The distribution of girls and boys is atypical for the school. The school has received additional computer equipment and for one month you will have complete sets of equipment for your class's use. You have noticed that the girls are becoming increasingly timid in their use of all forms of practical equipment in class. The boys are becoming more dominant.

Scenario 3: The first-year group has taken responsibility for mounting an environmental studies exhibition for the whole school. You are responsible for oversight of the exhibition. It will receive a lot of publicity and involve parental visits, visits from school governors, advisers, and education officers. In the last week before the launch you are very short of major exhibits. A fifth-year boy, whom you have been helping because of his discipline problems in school and lack of support at home, brings to you his collection of pressed flowers. You are astonished that he has an interest in this hobby and you fear for the reaction of his peers but know that he needs a boost to his self-esteem.

Scenario 4: Bus duty is an agreed duty and part of directed time for all staff. Your duty is shared with three other staff. For the past two weeks you have failed to turn up for your duty. Once you forgot, the other time you were unwell. It is the morning of your evening duty session and all three of your partners confront you openly in the staffroom about your lack of support.

Scenario 5: You have been acting teacher-in-charge of _____ for two terms. You applied for the substantive post when it was advertised but were not called for interview. A teacher from outside the school has been appointed and will take up post at the beginning of next term. You are still being paid the acting allowance and carrying the post until she arrives.

Scenario 6: Your assessment records show that most of your class are on target to match the expected attainment targets for their appropriate key stage. The standardised assessment tasks results also confirm your expectations but the national test results show wide variations from your patterns of pupil attainment. Next week you represent your school at the local group assessment moderation meeting.

Scenario 7: You are a D-allowance holder responsible for language work throughout the school. The whole school has considerable difficulties recruiting and holding on to teachers. Two of the staff responsible to you are underperforming. Parental complaints are now quite frequent and there is talk of pupil withdrawal and relocation.

Scenario 8: As reception class teacher you are at the front line of the National Curriculum implementation. Your pupils will be assessed at seven years, but many of them do not speak English as their first language. You are anxious that their attainment will not properly reflect their potential or the quality of your teaching.

Scenario 9: You are about to start your second year of teaching. During your probationary year, which you passed, you had a number of clashes with pupils in 2BN when you had to cover them for staff absence. Your new timetable shows that you will have 3BN last two periods on Friday afternoon from September onwards.

Continua

Continua represent a line of change or development from one stated position to another. The ends of continua are not necessarily opposites; they merely represent two stated positions. The points between are not described, these must be defined by the users who see themselves relative

to the two end statements whether at one of these positions or some-
where in between.

Continua also allow their users to chart change by keeping records of
earlier responses for comparison with later ones.

When considering each of the continua in this activity take time to
analyse the detail of your personal position and write out a statement to
describe it.

The following continua may be used selectively or as a whole set.
Ideally they should form part of a dialogue with a trusted colleague, a
basis for sharing personal insights. They may also be effectively used in
a reciprocal manner where you complete a set based upon your perceptions of your colleague while she does the same for you.

The example below illustrates how continua are used.

I feel smokers have a personal right to smoke and should exert their right and smoke when they feel like it.	I feel smokers are a health hazard to themselves and others and legislation should be introduced to ban smoking.

The point indicated perhaps represents a person who is not in favour of
smoking but who does recognise the personal rights of individuals and
is not in favour of an enforced ban.

1 I keep an open mind about pupils and their behaviour and potential. — I assess pupils and tend to retain my view of their behaviour and potential.

2 I listen well to pupils and colleagues and respond with sensitivity. — I find it difficult to be a good listener and sensitive respondent.

3 I see my work and my contribution in the context of the overall work of the school. — I see my work and contribution solely in the context of my own efforts.

4 If I do not get my own way and feel that others are wrong I become very difficult for other staff to relate to. — If I do not get my own way and feel others are wrong I work hard in a reasonable manner to persuade others to see my point of view.

5 I see myself as an independent agent functioning alone.

I see myself as a member of a group functioning together with colleagues.

6 In a group I am dismissive of other people's views and insensitive to their feelings.

In a group I am aware of other people's views and sensitive to their feelings.

7 In my classroom teaching I am constantly on the move interacting with pupils.

In my teaching I am often passive once the class is settled to the tasks I have set.

8 I have a regular routine of lessons based on my well-proven scheme of work.

I have a clear overview of what I am doing but am flexible in planning lessons to take account of developments in class.

9 The activities I provide for pupils are always well structured to fit the time and resources available.

The activities I provide leave space for pupils to add their own insights and directions.

10 In my teaching I am preoccupied to cover the agreed schemes of work and ensure the pupils know this work well.

In my teaching I am concerned to help my pupils to see the connection between my work and that of other teachers.

11 I have a limited range of teaching styles which I use in a well tried and regular manner.

I have a wide range of styles and am flexible to match these to emerging situations.

12 In class I focus attention on those pupils who clearly demonstrate that they need my help.

In class I aim to be aware of the needs of all pupils not just those whose needs are demonstrable.

13 I see my role to develop pupil knowledge and skill and do not become involved in their personal or social development.

└───────────┘

I see my role encompassing pupil development of knowledge, skill, personal attributes and social ability.

14 I have my classroom rules and enforce them rigidly.

└───────────┘

I believe the pupils should help to develop classroom rules and share responsibility for their enforcement.

15 Class control is entirely my responsibility and I never ask for help.

└───────────┘

Class control is the responsibility of all the staff and I regularly request help.

16 I display pupils' best work as a means of reinforcing their efforts and demonstrating good standards.

└───────────┘

I display the work of all pupils with their assistance to reinforce all their efforts.

17 I am confident in my range of subject knowledge.

└───────────┘

I have distinct anxieties about my range of subject knowledge.

18 I am aware of the range of ability in my classes and take this into account when preparing materials and planning lessons.

└───────────┘

I recognise the difficulties of teaching to pupils with a range of abilities and pitch my materials and planning at the middle ability to give all the pupils some chance of success.

19 When I mark my pupils' work I give them a sense of their attainment.

└───────────┘

When I mark my pupils' work I communicate with them about the work and demonstrate my personal interest in them.

20 I accept the need to keep parents well informed of the progress of their children but restrict my efforts to written reports.

└──────────────┘

I see the need for regular personal contact with parents to support them and help them to reinforce the work of school.

21 I am confident in my existing skills and knowledge and do not invest much time and effort in extending these.

└──────────────┘

I recognise the need to continue my personal development of new skills and knowledge.

22 I am a regular participant in in-service training.

└──────────────┘

I have little interest in in-service training.

When you have identified your position on those continua that you have used, write the date on the sheets and store the papers for later reference. Come back to the same continua after a year and check out your reactions again.

Likert scales

In this activity you are presented with statements covering many aspects of teaching. Against each statement is a scale 1–5. If you strongly agree that the statement describes you, then draw a ring around 5. If you strongly disagree, and the statement does not describe you, then draw a ring around 1. The value 3 accords with a neutral view of the statement.

As you work through the series analyse your personal view of each statement and write a note to sum up your own position.

If possible, carry out the activity with a trusted colleague, and re-member the activity can be done reciprocally: you complete an agreed set of statements for her while she completes the same set based upon her perceptions of you.

1 I am self-critical of my work.   1 2 3 4 5

2 I am committed to the growth and development of the whole school.   1 2 3 4 5

3 I shape the curriculum into plans for pupils' work.   1 2 3 4 5

4 I actively engage with learners as they work in the classroom.   1 2 3 4 5

5 I provide pupils with activities to practise their knowledge and skills.   1 2 3 4 5

6 I provide my pupils with problem-solving situations.   1 2 3 4 5

7 I provide a wide variety of learning experiences for my pupils.   1 2 3 4 5

8 I challenge my pupils to the limits of their ability.   1 2 3 4 5

9 I regularly talk with individual pupils about their work.   1 2 3 4 5

10 I regularly get my pupils thinking about the work they are doing.   1 2 3 4 5

11 I am an effective user of group work activities in my teaching.   1 2 3 4 5

12 I emphasise learning to learn in my approach to teaching.   1 2 3 4 5

13 I regularly organise problem-solving situations to encourage pupils to work together.   1 2 3 4 5

14 I am a teacher who is prepared to take risks in teaching.   1 2 3 4 5

15 I keep to a regular routine of classroom activity.   1 2 3 4 5

16 I ask interesting and challenging questions in class.   1 2 3 4 5

17 I keep a balance between direction of pupils' work and freedom for the pupils to pursue their own lines of thought.   1 2 3 4 5

18 I always provide encouragement for pupils.   1 2 3 4 5

19 I am often sarcastic and critical of pupils.   1 2 3 4 5

20 I like to provoke pupils into deeper thought about their work.   1 2 3 4 5

21 I am continuously aware of the need to evaluate the quality of work.   1 2 3 4 5

22 My teaching is part of a planned progression of learning for pupils.   1 2 3 4 5

23 I am constantly assessing pupils to assess their needs.   1 2 3 4 5

24 I keep thorough records of my pupils' attainment and progress.   1 2 3 4 5

25 I use pupils' work to illustrate what I want other pupils to achieve.   1 2 3 4 5

26 I am able to communicate with pupils at
   different levels dependent on their ability.   1 2 3 4 5

27 In class I am lively and demonstrate my interest
   in pupils.   1 2 3 4 5

28 My marking is up to date.   1 2 3 4 5

29 My marking carries constructive challenging
   comments for pupils.   1 2 3 4 5

30 I am an excellent listener with pupils.   1 2 3 4 5

31 My classroom display is always current and
   related to the development of the work in hand.   1 2 3 4 5

32 I have a good knowledge and understanding of
   modern testing procedures.   1 2 3 4 5

33 I have a good knowledge and understanding of
   pupil continuous assessment techniques.   1 2 3 4 5

34 I have good information, organisation and
   retrieval skills.   1 2 3 4 5

35 I have good knowledge and understanding of the
   National Curriculum.   1 2 3 4 5

36 My classroom is a caring and supportive
   environment.   1 2 3 4 5

37 I have high expectations of pupils.   1 2 3 4 5

38 I can command attention in class with ease.   1 2 3 4 5

39 I maintain a purposeful, relaxed, quiet working
   environment in class.   1 2 3 4 5

40 I expect pupils to listen to each other, and
   demonstrate this with the quality of my own
   listening.   1 2 3 4 5

41 I allow freedom of movement around my
   classroom.   1 2 3 4 5

42 I ensure that the classroom furniture is
   appropriately arranged for the work in hand.   1 2 3 4 5

43 I am a confident user of audio-visual aids.   1 2 3 4 5

44 I move around all parts of the classroom.   1 2 3 4 5

45 My lessons are planned and well organised.   1 2 3 4 5

46 My pupils always know the purpose of our
   lessons.   1 2 3 4 5

47 I provide homework linked to classwork.   1 2 3 4 5

48 My classroom environment is lively.   1 2 3 4 5

49 I search for ways of making the pupils feel they
   are succeeding.   1 2 3 4 5

50 I work to help pupils build on their successes.   1 2 3 4 5

51 I carefully reinforce the success of individuals by
   discussing their work with the class.   1 2 3 4 5

52 I have good personal antennae for pupils' on-
   task level of work.   1 2 3 4 5

53 I have a clear overview of the work of my
   teaching groups.   1 2 3 4 5

54 I regularly involve parents in the work of their
   children.   1 2 3 4 5

55 I have a good awareness of all aspects of the
   school's local community.   1 2 3 4 5

56 I am able to provide support and have good
   listening skills with parents.   1 2 3 4 5

57 I am confident to use other adults in my
   classroom teaching.   1 2 3 4 5

58 I keep up-to-date with my educational reading.   1 2 3 4 5

59 I keep a good balance between my work for
   school and time for my personal life.   1 2 3 4 5

60 I enjoy teaching and thrive on its challenges.   1 2 3 4 5

Summary

Together the activities in this chapter lead to a detailed and comprehensive insight into the professional work of teachers for teachers. Used in a systematic way they build up an effective record, and this is well illustrated in the next few pages by the compilation of some of the recording sheets related to classroom observation. When seen together they represent the objective evidence of personal performance that underpins teacher self-description in the appraisal situation. They are a way of guarding against inadequate appraisal by line managers whilst at the same time contributing positively to the personal and professional development of those who use them.

The following set of completed record sheets shows the range of ways in which a single lesson may be recorded.

CLASSROOM ACTIVITY/MOBILITY MAPPING SHEET

Name of class/teaching group ___ 3MN   date 4th Oct

record of activities

TIME	ACTIVITY	TIME	ACTIVITY
0	walking to class	30	checking books
1	walking, checking books	31	checking books
2	walking, checking books	32	introducing development of task
3	walking, class start to arrive	33	developing task
4	controlling class at door	34	developing task
5	controlling class, waiting for silence	35	assisting group with new task
6	settling class	36	assisting group with new task
7	talking to class about behaviours	37	responding to pupils' suggestions
8	reminding class about work for today	38	responding to pupils' suggestions
9	giving out books	39	whole class active, working well
10	giving out books	40	whole class active, working well
11	dealing with pupils A and B	41	whole class active, working well
12	dealing with pupils A and B	42	pupil unwell ©
13	dealing with pupils A and B	43	pupil unwell, class concerned
14	settling whole class	44	pupil unwell, A and B fighting
15	settling whole class	45	sorting out A and B: D talking C to no avail
16	introducing lesson	46	repositioned A in C's place
17	introducing lesson	47	talking at whole class re. behaviour
18	questioning class	48	regaining control and pattern of work
19	question/answers with class	49	full order restored, class working
20	question/answer, reinforcing control A&B	50	keeping close eye on B, class working
21	giving more information to class	51	keeping close eye on B, class working
22	giving more information to class	52	reinforcing future control over A
23	setting task for class	53	reinforcing future control over A
24	class active on task, checking	54	observing whole class, checking
25	checking, helping individuals	55	checking notes for next lesson
26	checking, helping individuals	56	checking notes for next lesson
27	reinforcing control over A and B	57	informing class about next lesson
28	reinforcing control over A and B	58	informing class about next lesson
29	checking books	59	informing class about next lesson

record of mobility

classroom perimeter

TEACHER TALK/PUPIL TALK RECORD SHEET

Name of class/teaching group ___3MN___   date ___4th Oct___

A. TEACHER TALK		B. PUPIL TALK		C. SILENCE	
starting time	amount of time	starting time	amount of time	starting time	amount of time
5.00	14 mins	19.00	2 mins.		
21.00	3 mins			24.00	8 mins
32.00	3 mins			35.00	2 mins
		37.00	2 mins	39.00	5 mins
44.00	6 mins			50.00	
57.00	3 mins.				
TOTAL 29 mins		TOTAL 4 mins		TOTAL 15 mins	

TYPES OF CLASSROOM TALK RECORD SHEET

Name of class/teaching group ___3MN___   date ___4th Oct___

TEACHER TALK

	Tally	TOTAL
Introducing work	✓✓✓✓✓	6
Giving instruction	✓✓✓	3
Exerting control	✓✓✓✓✓✓✓✓✓	10
Questioning	✓✓✓	3
Gaining attention	✓✓✓✓✓	6
Giving information	✓✓✓✓✓	6
Intervening between pupils	✓✓✓✓✓	5
Waiting / giving out books / checking	W W W B B B c c c c	11

PUPIL TALK

	Tally	TOTAL
Questioning teacher	✓✓✓✓✓	5
Pupil/pupil on-task talk	✓✓✓✓✓✓✓	7
Pupil/pupil off-task talk	✓✓✓✓✓	5
Answering teacher	✓✓✓✓	4
Pupil informing class		

PUPIL PURSUIT RECORD SHEET	pupil D/E

Name of class teaching group___3MN__ date 4ᵗʰ Oct

TIME	ACTIVITY
2.50	arrives late for lesson but first to arrive.
3.00	reading book seated at desk at back of class.
5.10	still reading book in secret, not attentive to teacher
9.00	shows interest in books being given out.
9.15	returned to reading story book in secret
16.10	now starts to listen to teacher
19.10	asks question and gets response from teacher, remains attentive
24.30	starts reading story book again in secret
25.50	sees teacher approaching, hides book and works to task
26.00	teacher checking work. asks question and gets answer
26.45	returns to story book as teacher moves away.
32.00	listens to teacher attentively talking at front of class
34.10	working to task set by teacher, continues working
43.05	distracted by pupil C's illness
44.15	watching teacher dealing with pupils A and B
47.20	listening to teacher
48.40	return to story book, reading in secret
57.15	puts story book away, listening to teacher
60.	leaves classroom with rest of pupils.

TIME	ACTIVITY
\multicolumn{2}{c}{PUPIL PURSUIT RECORD SHEET pupil DL}

TIME	ACTIVITY
\multicolumn{2}{l}{PUPIL PURSUIT RECORD SHEET pupil DL}
\multicolumn{2}{l}{Name of class teaching group __3MN__ date 4th Oct}
3.15	Arrives late for lesson. One of first to arrive.
3.30	Sorting out books
4.00	Listening attentively to teacher
9.15	Checking book received from teacher
10.05	Talking quietly to neighbour
11.00	watching teacher deal with A and B
14.00	Listening to teacher
19.10	Questioning teacher / listening to teacher's answer
20.50	Listening carefully. full attention on teacher
23.10	working independently on set task
30.40	checking something with neighbour
32.00	Listening to teacher
35.00	working independently again
42.00	neighbour unwell, concerned
45.00	leave room with C to visit medical room.
	Does not return to class

SINGLE LESSON TIME LINE RECORD SHEET

Name of class/teaching group _____ date _____

BEFORE THE LESSON

Objectives : Distribute books and materials in orderly manner. Describe set tasks and organise pupils' work in pairs Complete written tasks. Control pupils A and B effectively

Planned outcomes : Each pupil will have completed ten assignments in pairs . and answered set questions. Pupils will be able to describe three basic fact about expansion A and B to complete same tasks.

Particular notes/Points for attention : Insufficient desks for all pupils, five need to sit facing windows at back of classroom. Need to reinforce control over A and B.

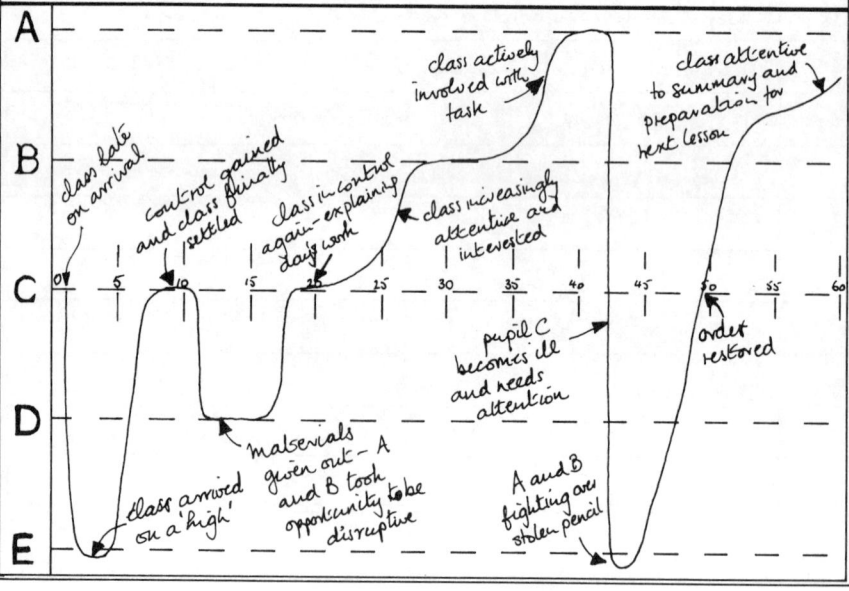

DAY'S TIME LINE   OVERVIEW/PLANNING SHEET

date 4th Oct

PRE-REGISTRATION SESSION   go over details of lesson, check materials and equipment. See head teacher, remind her of agreement not to include me in cover arrangements

REGISTRATION/ASSEMBLY

Register tutor group. Final check on plans for morning's lessons.

SESSION 1   1st year combined science: Materials. Working in threes, pupils to experience whole range of available materials to identify similarities and differences. Use odd one out game to reinforce idea of properties of materials. All pupils to complete assignment sheet 4. Check that all pupils are actively involved.

SESSION 2   5th year GCSE Biology: Structure of the Human Eye. Go over previous work, use models of the eye to reinforce information on structure and functions. Hand out 20 basic facts sheets. Use initial factual recall test to conclude work on the eye. Hand out information sheets on the human ear.

LUNCH BREAK

Fill in time lines for morning session
Help technician to set up expansion materials for 3rd year

SESSION 3   3rd year low ability group: Expansion. Circus arrangement of investigation in pairs. Ten sets of equipment with illustrated instruction cards. Give out recording sheets. Pairs to complete a single record of their combined work. Check on 3 basic facts about expansion.

SESSION 4   6th form tutorial session: A level Biology Go over assignment 5 with JN and CB. Check progress on assignment reports for whole group. Remind DL of interview dates and deadlines for applications. Discuss work problems with VN and possible alternative courses.

AFTER-SCHOOL SESSION

Fill in time lines for afternoon sessions
meet DK to compare work and discuss time lines

DAY'S TIME LINE RECORD SHEET

Name of class / teaching groups 1 DJ : 5ᵗʰ GCSE : 3 MN : 6ᵗʰ Tutorial date 4ᵗʰ Oct

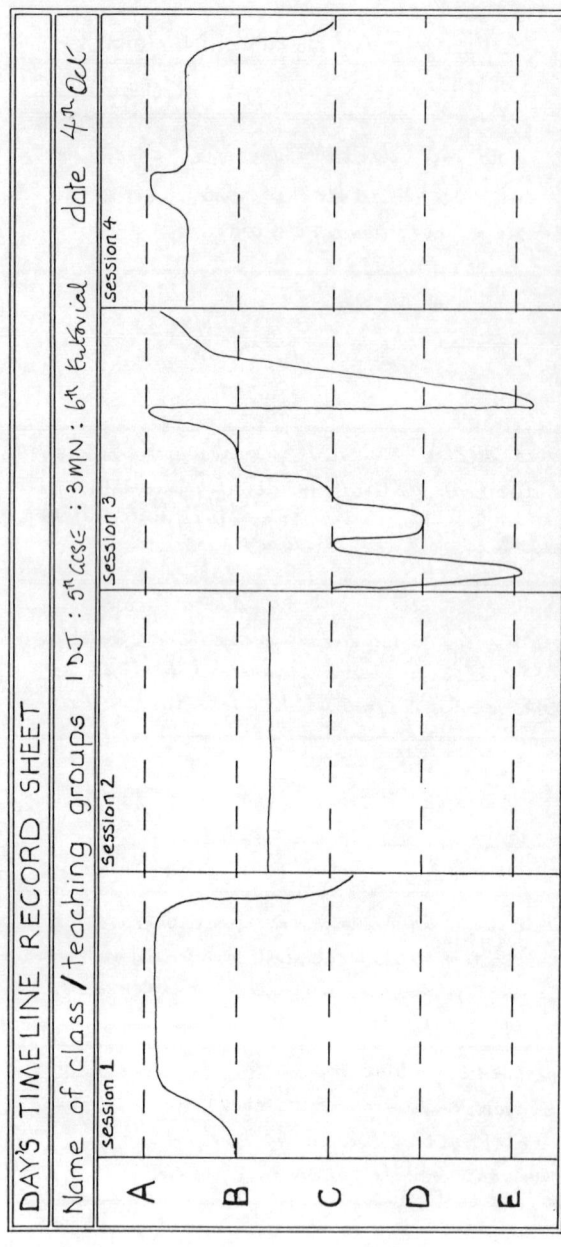

	Session 1	Session 2	Session 3	Session 4
A				
B				
C				
D				
E				

Session 1 not all materials ready for start of lesson, everyone worked well but insufficient time to round off the lesson and complete assignment sheets, hence dip in line.

Session 2 well motivated group but uninspired lesson. Needs greater practical input. Possibly need to return to direction of eye again

Session 3 See more detailed explanation on sheet 'Single lesson Time line Record Sheet'

Session 4 very good session until counselling VN went badly wrong. Need to follow this up urgently.

6 How can I practise?

This chapter provides you with a range of opportunities and ideas to enable you to gain experience in using many of the tools of appraisal. None is intended as a final, formal document or scheme. It is vital that you take the ideas, concepts and tools provided and adapt them for your own or your school's use.

> **Remember**
> You can photocopy, use or adapt any of the tools in this section. They are starting points for your own development.

Design and write your own open report

* pupil achievement
* teaching skills
* classroom climate
* essential records
* relationships
* organisation/administration
* meeting involvement/teamwork
* preparation for teaching
* what has happened in the last y

As a starting point for self-appraisal:

- Design an open report form for yourself
- Fill it in.

The personal report can be as detailed as you choose but in the first instance ensure that:

- You take a *broad* view of yourself as a teacher
- You take an *objective* view.

As can be seen from the diagram, this initial appraisal could become very detailed covering many areas. That is not the intent of this starting point. The intent is to make an attempt at a general overview of performance in a more objective manner. Additional detail will be available in other tools as you move through the chapter.

Essential records

This section should always provide your base-line of information, and will resemble the information available, in most cases, on an application form for employment. This should be updated each year and provide you with an excellent and readily available curriculum vitae.

- Name, address, telephone number
- Universities/colleges attended, dates, courses followed
- Qualifications gained
- Previous experience before present post — detail the experiences here with age groups taught, subject experience, pastoral experience, specific responsibilities accepted or projects undertaken
- Present job description, responsibilities and salary scale
- In-service training: courses attended, courses led; INSET provided for colleagues in school; aftercare provided for colleagues in school
- Management responsibility: experience of implementing new systems, organisational arrangements, schemes of work, etc.

Base record — last academic year

This sheet should be filled in in detail as it provides the base on which you undertake your appraisal. The completed sheet should be appended each year to the essential records sheet.

Base record

- Academic year
- Teaching commitment — subject/class group
- Work undertaken for public examinations, assessment arrangements, standardised assessment tasks, reviews

- Pastoral responsibility
- INSET attended during the year: (a) in directed time; (b) voluntarily
- INSET — contribution made: (a) support provided for other teachers; (b) co-ordination of staff training
- Extra-curricular activities
- Involvement (formally) with parents/governors/community
- School journeys
- Any other activities/projects not covered.

Organisation and administration

In this and the following section why not *check* your initial response by undertaking a little evaluation, and why not *rate* response with a cross on the scale:

Excellent └─────────────────────────────────┘ Very poor

Always ensure that you have a space for comment/observation in your record keeping.

Attendance: Precisely how many sessions have I missed each term? For what reason? └────────┘

Punctuality: to school └────────┘
to the lesson settings └────────┘

Do I really arrive 'just on time'? Do I have time to have a few words with colleagues, to prepare my room? └────────┘

Personal Planning: Do I have clear short- and long-term objectives for my classes/pupils? └────────┘

When teaching a lesson can I look into my planning notes and easily see where it fits into the overall programme? └────────┘

Does planning take into account the needs of individual pupils? └────────┘

Personal record keeping: Do I keep an adequate record of the outcome of teaching sessions; of resources needed and used; of interaction with colleagues? └────────┘

Pupils record keeping: Do I keep detailed, accurate, objective records of pupils' work and progress? └_____┘

Do I provide opportunities for pupils to comment upon/add to their personal records? └_____┘

Pupils with special educational needs: Do I make specific provision for such pupils related to their statements of need, or to their known needs if they have not been statemented? └_____┘

Equalising opportunities: Do I recognise any gender or race bias in my work? └_____┘

Do I make positive attempts to overcome any personal bias? └_____┘

Remember
At times we need to check our views carefully. On the three items below why not select a week at random during the past term and then check all three sets of records for the week. How much planning and recording did you actually do? Was it adequate?

Teacher administration: all the formal Local Authority and individual school administration returns └_____┘

Teacher duties: Have I carried out all other staff procedures appropriately — playground duty, cover, corridor duty? └_____┘

Classroom/resource organisation: Have I efficiently and effectively made my classroom a resource base? Do I manage resources so that they last throughout the year? Are they well stored? Are my teaching bases tidy, well looked after by pupils? Are they lively centres with good displays? └_____┘

Do I use pupils' work as an integral part of classroom display? └─────────────┘

Do I provide appropriate stimuli through the use of effective classroom display? └─────────────┘

Teaching skills

Skills in this area can be categorised into these main headings:

- preparation
- interaction
- follow-up.

Again, all sections need a set of questions to attempt to gain an *objective* view of how a teacher is functioning. Build up the questions for yourself for this section onwards.

Lesson/group/pupil preparation	└─────────────┘
Resource preparation	└─────────────┘
Pupil/group/class discipline	└─────────────┘
Teacher presentation — content and quality of work	└─────────────┘
Pupil presentation — content and quality of work	└─────────────┘
Marking	└─────────────┘
Report writing	└─────────────┘
Examination/assessment results	└─────────────┘

It is well worth while, on occasion, taking a random sample of pupils' work and then working through it to make notes on the efficiency of marking, the quality of presentation, and then checking pupil reports to ensure that the work undertaken was accurately represented in the termly/annual report.

Relationships

- with teaching staff — peers └─────────────┘
  - managers └─────────────┘
  - subordinates └─────────────┘
- with non-teaching staff — administrative └─────────────┘
  - teaching support └─────────────┘
- with pupils — different age groups └─────────────┘
  - in different settings └─────────────┘
- with parents — formal setting inside and outside parents' evenings └─────────────┘

— casual contact/informal contact ⌴
- with support agencies — educational psychologists ⌴
  — social workers ⌴
  — careers ⌴
  — other ⌴
- with members of the community ⌴
- in a team setting — staff meetings ⌴
  — working groups ⌴
  — pastoral ⌴
  — cross-faculty ⌴

Areas of consideration here: Am I aware of the meeting procedures? Do I contribute? Do I lead? Can I aid concensus?

Open report

On the basis of the information you have recorded, now *write* your own open report. If your view of yourself is accurate this is the sort of report you could expect your teacher manager to write as an annual appraisal report, or indeed be the sort of reference you would be provided with. When writing the report also keep the following questions in mind:

- What are the particular strengths and talents I have?
- In what areas do I feel I need additional support?
- Would I be glad of support and advice in any areas?
- Would I happily undertake INSET courses in any of the areas?
- What effect has the school had in helping me in areas of strength or weakness?
- Are there any objectives for change that I would set immediately to ensure an improved performance?

This starting point for appraisal helps the global view the teacher has of herself and should give a view of:

- Who am I?
- What do I do for a living?
- What are the major aspects of my job?
- How am I doing in them?

Am I accurate in my self-perception?

Even when involved in self-evaluation it is important at some stage to test your perceptions of yourself against the view that others have of you.

For this exercise it is suggested that you gain the involvement of a trusted colleague and undertake the exercise jointly.

Remember
The trusted colleague can be your teacher manager. It does not have to be someone of the same status.

---

1 Complete the assessment forms in regard to your perceptions of yourself and also in regard to your perceptions of your colleague.
2 Ask her to do the same.
3 Spend some time discussing the outcomes of the assessments. Discuss in detail where views are different, and attempt to pinpoint actual issues on which perceptions have been built.

This exercise does intend to ensure that you talk to a colleague about your performance in a structured way. It also intends to provide a starting point for you to test your perceptions of yourself against others.

You may well wish to change or adapt some of the indicators of performance in the chart to ensure that they adequately reflect your own specific post.

How to evaluate your own staff meetings

Much of the development work that goes on in schools is undertaken in sub- or working groups. It is very rare for a member of staff not to have responsibility for leading in at least a small group setting. It is in such settings that essential management skills are developed and it is vital for teachers and teacher managers to have a clear view of their performance. It is often in these small (or large) staff group meetings that teachers will 'form a view' of their colleagues.

A successful appraisal of a staff meeting setting is not merely a function of the 'handling skills' within the meeting. It is very much also a function of the efficiency of the organisation of the meeting.

1 Use the evaluation sheet to help you plan and appraise your own handling of meetings.
2 Share it with a trusted colleague, once you are more confident, to get a second view of your handling and organisation of such groups.
3 Where you help to appraise other members of staff, share the schedule with them and utilise it to assist in the improvement of quality for all meetings.

PERFORMANCE ASSESSMENT

Indicators of performance A	Rating scale			Indicators of performance B	Objective observations in this area
	A Applies	Average	B Applies		
Very interested in work				Not very interested in work	
Keen and energetic				Lacking enthusiasm	
Makes positive responses to all issues				Likely to be negative	
Very dependable				Unreliable	
Very hardworking				Does the minimum required	
Good standard of dress				Untidy or uncaring in dress	
Has good subject or academic knowledge				Poor subject or academic knowledge	
Good knowledge of individual pupils				Does not know pupils well	

Works well on own initiative						Requires supervision
Easily approachable for other members of staff						Difficult to approach for staff members
Easily approachable for pupils						Difficult to approach for pupils
Cooperative with peers and teacher managers						Uncooperative with peers and teacher managers
Confident in all aspects of work						Unable to present in confident manner
Well respected by a wide range of people						Not generally well respected
Good quality of written work						Poor written work
Large volume of work undertaken						Little evidence of quantity of work
Good discipline with individual pupils						Poor discipline with individual pupils

PERFORMANCE ASSESSMENT — continued

Indicators of performance — A	Rating scale A Applies	Average	B Applies	Indicators of performance — B	Objective observations in this area
Good discipline with large groups of pupils				Poor discipline with large groups of pupils	
Judgement usually reliable				Judgement unreliable	
Makes sound decisions				Makes unsound decisions	
Good leadership skills				Lacks leadership skills	
Appears fair in handling pupils and staff				Appears biased and unfair in handling staff and pupils	
Finds original ways to move forward				No indication of original thought	
Able to delegate well in appropriate settings				Not able to delegate, or inappropriate delegation	
Able to put points over clearly and effectively				Communicates poorly	

Schedule for evaluation of staff/sub-group/working party meetings

ISSUE	AGENDA ITEM NUMBER	OBSERVATIONS
Opportunity for all staff to contribute to agenda?		
Agenda circulated in good time?		
Relevant documentation circulated in advance	Item 1) 2) Specific 3) items 4) only 5) etc	
Were all relevant people in attendance on time?	Specific people for timed agenda items Item 1) 2) Specific 3) items etc	Apologies:
Were minutes taken? By whom?		
Was the time allocated to the meeting appropriate for the agenda?		
Outcomes of actions agreed at last meeting		
How were individual agenda items presented	Lead person on items (all) Item 1) 2) 3) etc	
Was discussion on each item adequate? Did all members express views? Did some dominate?	Item 1) (all) 2) 3) etc	
Has summing up on items focussed on important issues?	Item 1) (all) 2) 3) etc	
Has agreement been reached?	Item 1) (all) 2) 3) etc	

Schedule for Evaluation — continued

ISSUE	AGENDA ITEM NUMBER	OBSERVATIONS
Have confidential items been properly addressed?	Specific items noted	
Has there been agreement on action to be taken — by whom/the scale/reporting back?	All items	
Were written minutes sent out quickly? Were they clear and accurate?		
Has an action plan been circulated with/as part of the minutes?	All items	
Have confidential items been appropriately recorded on minutes? How are these items recorded?	Specific items	
Have items been noted in minutes to carry forward to next staff meeting?		
Has time/date been set for call for items for next agenda?		

Recruit your perfect replacement

One of the keys to self-appraisal is a detailed understanding of exactly what is expected of you! This exercise attempts to help you clarify:

- What is expected of you
- What skills you require to do the job
- How to play your part appropriately in any selection procedure

It does this by asking you to organise the recruitment of your perfect replacement. You do this by going through the following stages:

Analyse exactly what you do now

Use the framework below to analyse the job that is now being expected of you.

AREA	RESPONSIBILITIES	% TIME SPENT
ADMINISTRATION Position held		
Responsibility allowance		
Position of responsibility or delegated responsibilities		
TEACHING Subjects taught		
Classes taught		
Public examinations and assessments for which you prepared pupils		
Pastoral/tutor group responsibility		
Responsible for development in subject/pastoral areas		
Staff management responsibility		
Resource allocation responsibility		
INSET Responsibility for INSET within school		
Responsibility for INSET within LEA		
Membership of examination boards or assessment panels		

RELATIONSHIPS
Responsibility for relationships with:
    parents
    governors
    outside agencies		

Responsibility for extra-curricular activities		

Writing a job description

Having made an analysis of *all* that you do, now write a *job description* for your post.

Person specification for post of — (example given for headteacher of primary school)

REQUIREMENTS: M = minimum I = ideal	Application	Reference	Interview
1 QUALIFICATIONS			
M Qualified Teacher status	✓		
M Degree	✓		
I Higher Degree	✓		
I Management training specification	✓		
2 EXPERIENCE			
M Seven years' teaching experience	✓		
M Two years' experience as deputy head	✓	✓	
M Indication of regular attendance at long and short INSET courses	✓		
3 KNOWLEDGE			
M Detailed knowledge of National Curriculum, programmes of study, attainment targets, and assessment arrangements.	✓	✓	✓
M Detailed knowledge of child development	✓		✓
M Detailed knowledge of modern management training initiatives	✓	✓	✓
I Detailed knowledge of local management of schools and local financial management	✓		✓
4 SKILLS			
M Evidence of leadership qualities			✓
M Evidence of experience in organising and offering INSET — school based	✓	✓	
I Evidence of experience in organising and offering INSET — LEA-wide and nationally	✓	✓	
M Evidence of organisational ability within the primary school setting			✓
M Able to write clearly for different audiences	✓		✓
M Able to communicate orally to different audiences			✓
5 SPECIFIC COMMITMENTS REQUIRED BY SCHOOL			
M Commitment to team teaching	✓		✓
I Willing to live within the catchment area of the school			✓
I Willing to work in the evenings to support a community policy			✓

Remember
A job description only has to list the *main* duties and responsibilities of the post.

You do not have to make an exhaustive list of a teacher's full professional obligations. A job description does allocate duties and responsibilities but does not direct any particular amount of time to be spent on carrying them out. A job description should:

1 Enable a better match to be made between applicant and post.
2 Provide a base from which to derive selection criteria.
3 Let a candidate know what the main core of the job is within the overall school framework.
4 Provide consistent information for applicants.
5 Assist those involved in the selection procedure.

Writing a job or person specification

Now that you have written the job description you have to write the job specification. You have to identify the essential qualifications, experience, skills, knowledge or commitments that are required to ensure that the job can be carried out successfully.

It is also interesting and helpful to consider at what stage you would look to check such specifications — on the application forms, at the reference stage, or during the interview procedure.

The following page provides you with a starting point for developing such a job specification. Use it as a model to build up an appropriate job specification for your post.

Write an advertisement

Having now gained great clarity in regard to the job and its requirements, write an advertisement for the post. Use both local and national press advertisements as models and, keeping the cost in mind, attempt to write a succinct advertisement which will attract candidates with the correct skills. Your advertisement should include the advice that a visit to the school is essential prior to interview.

Structuring a visit

You have now reached the stage of having a group of candidates who wish to visit. Now structure the visits by responding to the questions below.

Remember
All candidates should have exactly the same opportunity.

---

1 Should candidates visit individually or in a group/groups?
2 How much time should be allocated for a visit?
3 Who should be the 'lead' member of staff arranging the visit?
4 Which members of staff should spend time with the candidates?
5 Do the members of staff selected know what information they are supposed to impart?
6 Does the member of staff selected know what information her colleagues are imparting?
7 Are any judgements being made about candidates during their visit? If so are they aware of that fact?
8 What chance do the candidates have to talk to other members of staff?
9 What opportunity do candidates have to raise any issues of concern which they may have?
10 Will candidates be asked questions about their visit during the interview? If so are they aware of that fact?

Organising an interview

There are many aspects involved in organising an interview. You are only going to be concerned with one aspect, writing and structuring the questions.

1 Write out what you feel to be the *ten* most important questions to ask candidates at interview for your post.
2 Give each question a weighting scale of 1 to 3
   a) Vital they answer clearly, correctly. Failure to do so may indicate an inability to do the job. These are normally questions of a 'technical' nature.
   b) Important that the framework of the response is correct, but the question allows some interpretation in the answers.
   c) Questions which search out the individual's personal views on a range of issues.

7 Outcomes

We have now reached the stage where we need to ask the crucial question: 'What will be the outcomes of the work I undertake on self-appraisal?'

We shall look at the outcomes in terms of three areas:

a) Personal outcomes
b) School outcomes
c) Pupil outcomes.

Personal outcomes

Successful self-appraisal should impinge on four key areas:

1 It should improve the quality of teaching and relationships.
2 It should improve motivation towards the work.
3 It should improve a teacher's ability to manage and support others through being more aware of herself.
4 It should improve a teacher's ability to contribute to a school appraisal scheme.

Remember
Benefits such as these are not only beneficial to a teacher in her present post, but are significant *career* enhancement skills.

It might be helpful to consider self-appraisal as a hurdles race! Each time you clear a hurdle you have both put another potential problem behind you and moved closer to a successful finish.

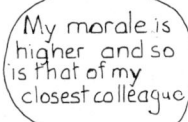

My morale is higher and so is that of my closest colleague

I'm more aware of the criteria required to be a good teacher.

I'm not anxious any more about school or Authority appraisal schemes.

I'm not waiting for a crisis or an instruction to change what I'm doing. I'm looking to see how I can improve.

I'm being judged more on what I do in the classroom, rather than what I'm perceived to do around the school.

Parents of my pupils seem to recognise that I'm working hard to be a good teacher

I'm able to have more helpful, meaningful discussions with colleagues.

I feel my pupils are getting a better quality teaching and learning.

Members of staff and school governors seem to appreciate the efforts I'm making.

School outcomes

One of the reasonable questions that most teachers will ask in regard to any appraisal system is: 'If I make a great effort to evaluate what I am doing, identify my training needs and improve my performance, what has the school got to offer me in return?'

It must be stressed that these should not be seen in terms of *rewards*, but as the school ensuring that there is a structured system both to encourage and enhance self-development.

Remember
For any method of appraisal to be a success it must be seen as a two-way support system.

$$teacher \rightleftharpoons school$$

A teacher will always be able to appraise herself in a more effective way when the school as a whole regularly appraises all it does.

The appraisal of different aspects of work within any school will be more effective, accurate, supportive and developmental when it includes the appraisal of the work being undertaken by individual teachers.

Remember
Do not see 'school outcomes' as a system of rewards.

Pupil outcomes

It is appropriate in a book such as this to end by asking: 'How will the pupils benefit from all of this?' We must never forget that everything we do is to enhance the quality of learning for our youngsters.

Remember
The work that children do and the way that they undertake it are key indicators to teacher performance.

It is also important to remember that pupils will be quick to recognise when a teacher is working hard to support them, to appraise what is going on and to improve her own performance. It does not matter too

What can the school offer in outcomes?

study leave
parttime
full-time

secondment
to other
employment

staff
exchanges

conference
attendance

full staff
conferences
and
seminars

structure
staff
handbooks

team
work

research
work

Write
development
papers

Supervising
other
staff

inducting
new
staff

Serving
on
committees

Serving
on
working
parties

planning
in-service
courses

providing
in-service
courses

recognition
responsibility
within the
Authority

job
rotation

negotiating
job
description

all are within your reach

What can the school offer you in outcomes?

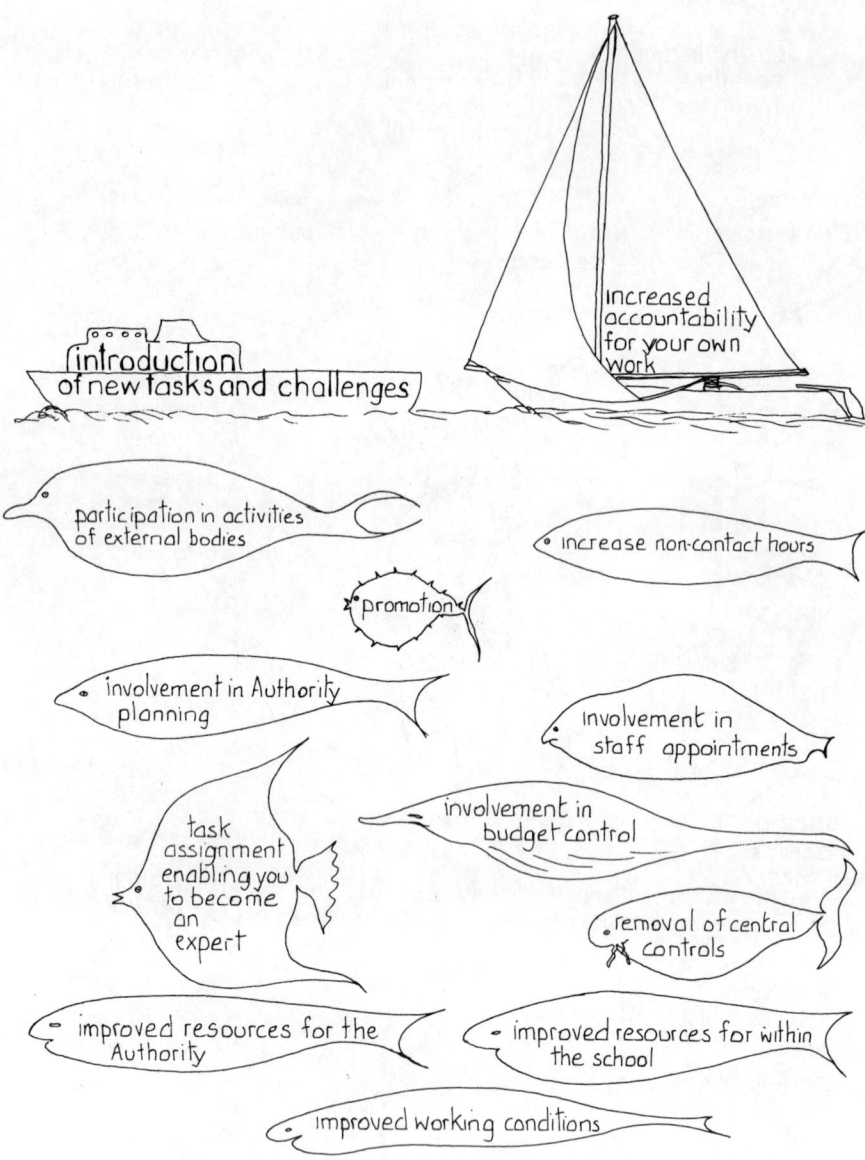

increased
accountability
for your own
work

introduction
of new tasks and challenges

participation in activities
of external bodies

increase non-contact hours

promotion

involvement in Authority
planning

involvement in
staff appointments

involvement in
budget control

task
assignment
enabling you
to become
an
expert

removal of central
controls

improved resources for the
Authority

improved resources for within
the school

improved working conditions

much which individual aspects teachers attempt to appraise, there is likely to be general as well as specific improvement in the quality of teaching where an individual becomes more aware of the job she is doing. A greater awareness of what is going on in the classroom plus a willingness to appraise areas of work in detail should show considerable change in areas such as:

- preparation of work
- presentation of lessons
- quality of relationships with pupils
- evaluation of work being done by pupils
- quality of recording pupils' progress
- quality of display of pupils' work.

In mathematical terms it should be the one occasion where:

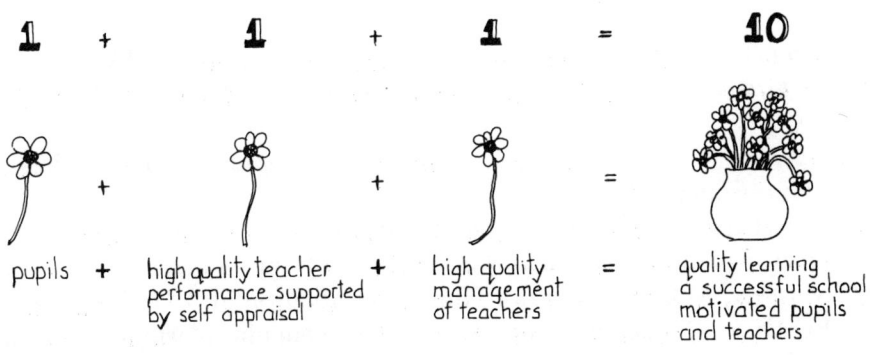

$$1 \quad + \quad 1 \quad + \quad 1 \quad = \quad 10$$

pupils + high quality teacher performance supported by self appraisal + high quality management of teachers = quality learning a successful school motivated pupils and teachers

Where may you end up?

I'm getting a better view of my potential.
I'm getting feedback on what I'm doing.
I think I know the areas where I need more training.
I think my class group can achieve more than they are at present in some areas.
I think I can use my time better.
I think I can establish a school appraisal scheme, I've got some skills.

This is more accurate.
This is helpful
This is a good base for development.
Others can share their views and work with you.
This should help you be a better teacher.

References

1. John, D, *Leadership in Schools*, Heinemann, London, 1980.
2. McGregor, D, *The Human Side of Enterprise*, McGraw Hill, N.Y., 1960.
3. Stewart, V & A, *Practical Performance Appraisal*, Gower Press, Farnborough, 1977.
4. Hertzberg, F, 'One More Time: How Do You Motivate Employees?' *Harvard Business Review*, Jan.–Feb. 1968, pp. 53–61.
5. Maslow, AH, 'A Theory of Human Motivation' in VH Vroom and EU Deci, *Management and Motivation*, Penguin, Harmondsworth, 1979.

Books and articles for further reading

ACAS, 'Report of Working Group on Appraisal/Training', London Advisory, Conciliation and Arbitration Service, June 1986.

ACAS, 'School Teacher Appraisal: A National Framework. Report of the National Steering Group on The School Teacher Appraisal Pilot Study'. London Advisory, Conciliation and Arbitration Service, 1989.

Butterworth, I, 'The Appraisal of Teachers. Education Management Information Exchange'. Slough NFER.

Cambridge Institute of Education, Report of Evaluation on the School Teacher Appraisal Pilot Study, 1989.

Gerhaus, D, 'Those Having Torches ... Teacher Appraisal: A Study', Suffolk Education Department, Ipswich, 1985.

Griffiths, D, 'Evaluating the Assessors' in *Schoolmaster and Career Teacher*, November 1980 (pp. 18 & 19), and December 1980 (pp. 5–7).

McGregor, D, 'A Necessary look at Performance Appraisal', *Harvard Business Review*, Sept/Oct, 1972, pp. 133–138.

Stewart, V & Stewart, A, *Practical Performance Appraisal*, Gower Press, Farnborough, 1977.

Suffolk Education Authority, 'In The Light of Torches. Teacher Appraisal A Further Study', London, The Industrial Society, 1987.

Tyler, RM, 'Accountability and Teacher Performance' in Rubin, L., *The inservice Education of Teachers*, Allyn & Bacon, Boston, 1978.

NOTES

NOTES

NOTES

NOTES

NOTES

NOTES

NOTES

NOTES